STOP THE POLLUTION
& INSPIRE PEOPLE
TO PICK-UP
WHIPPED CREAM
CANISTERS
OF NITROUS OXIDE
JUNKIES
AND MAKE
ART

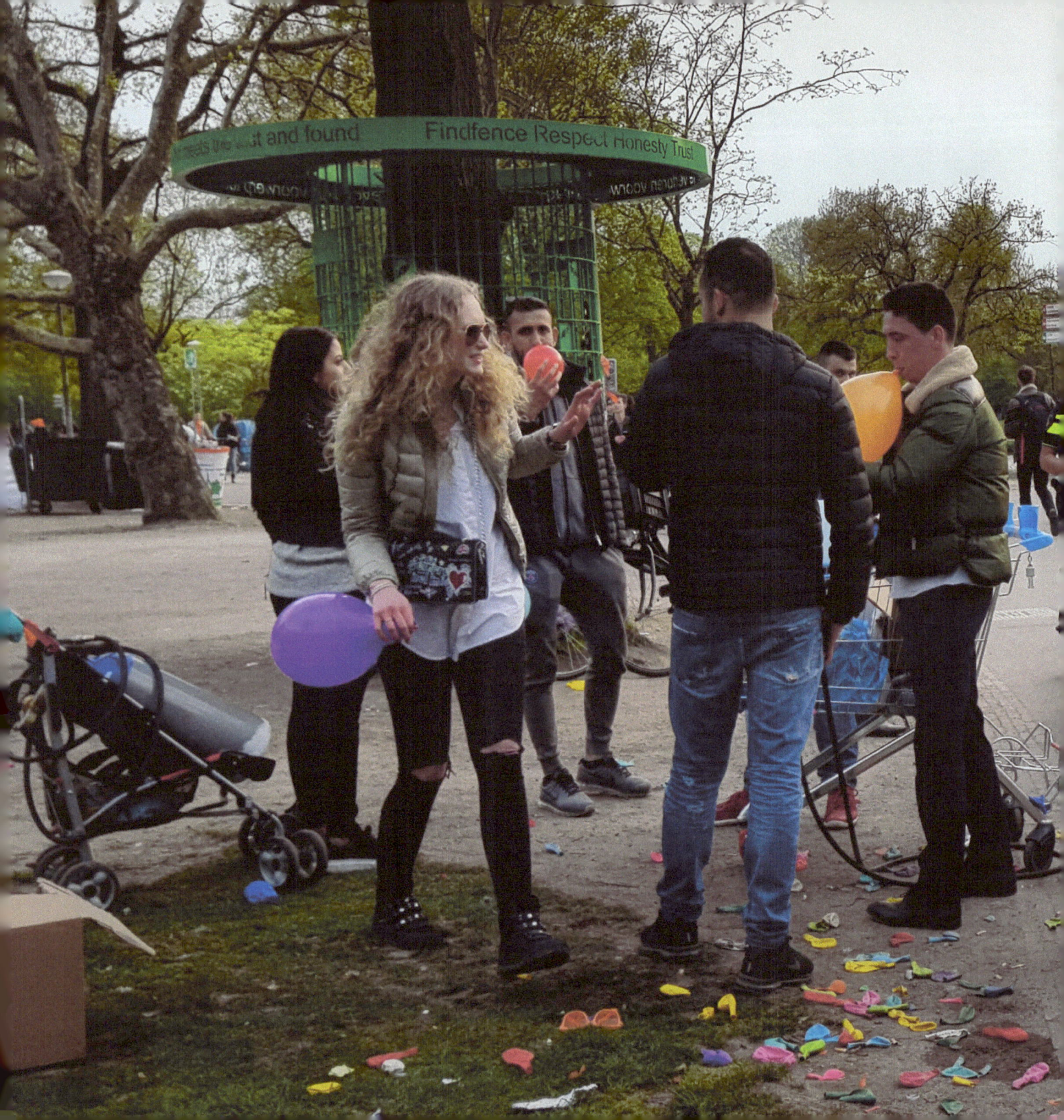

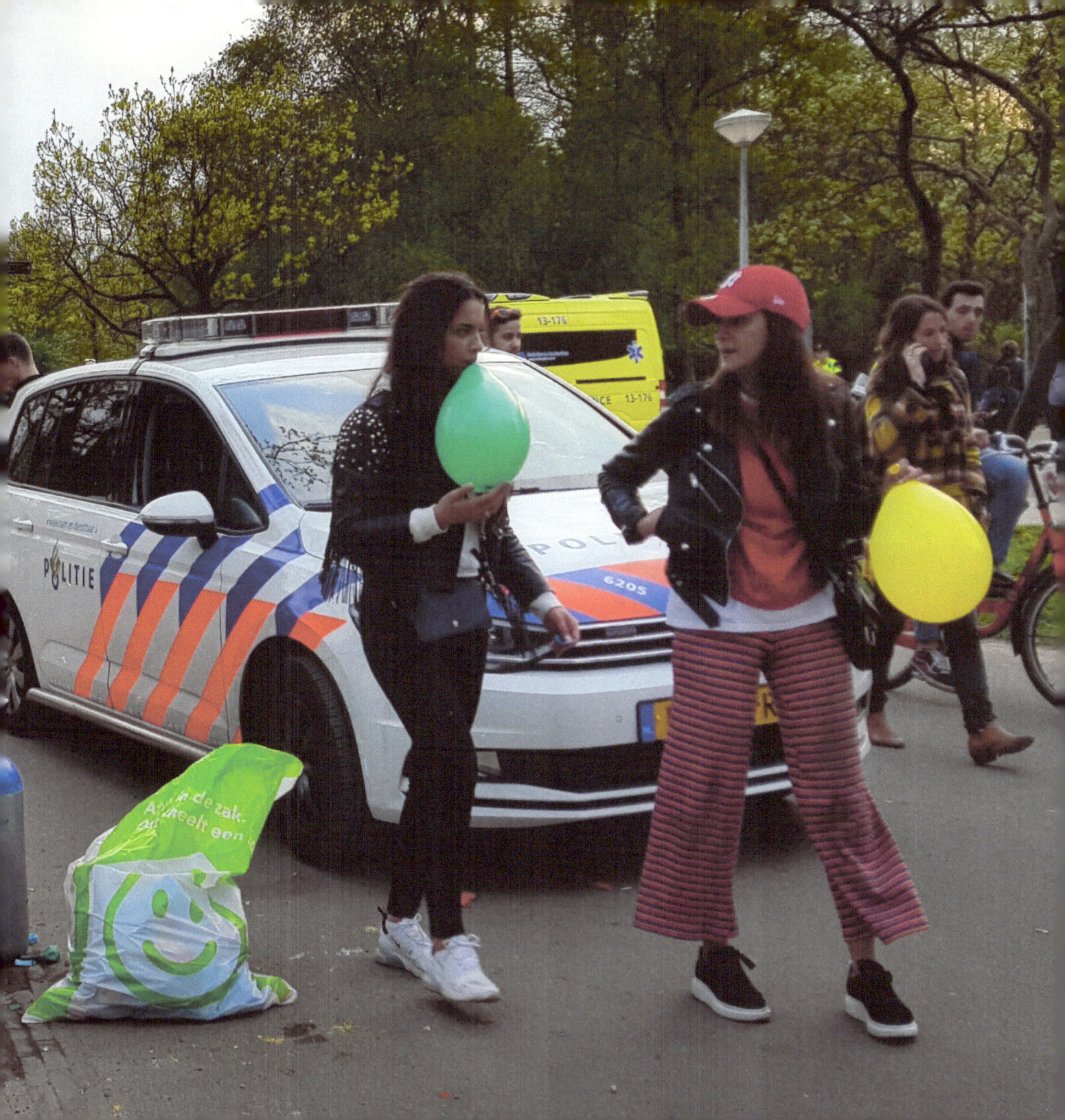

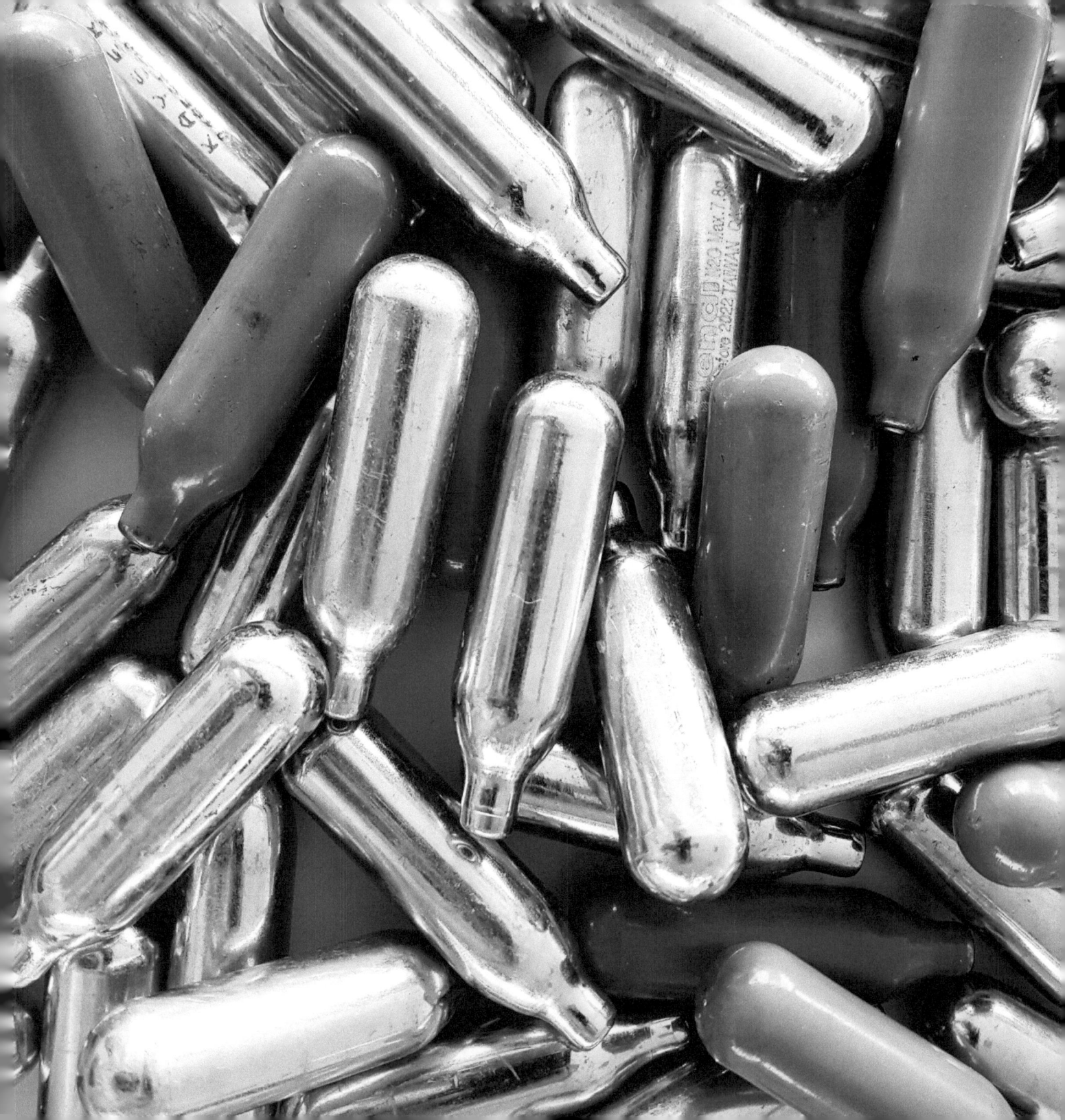

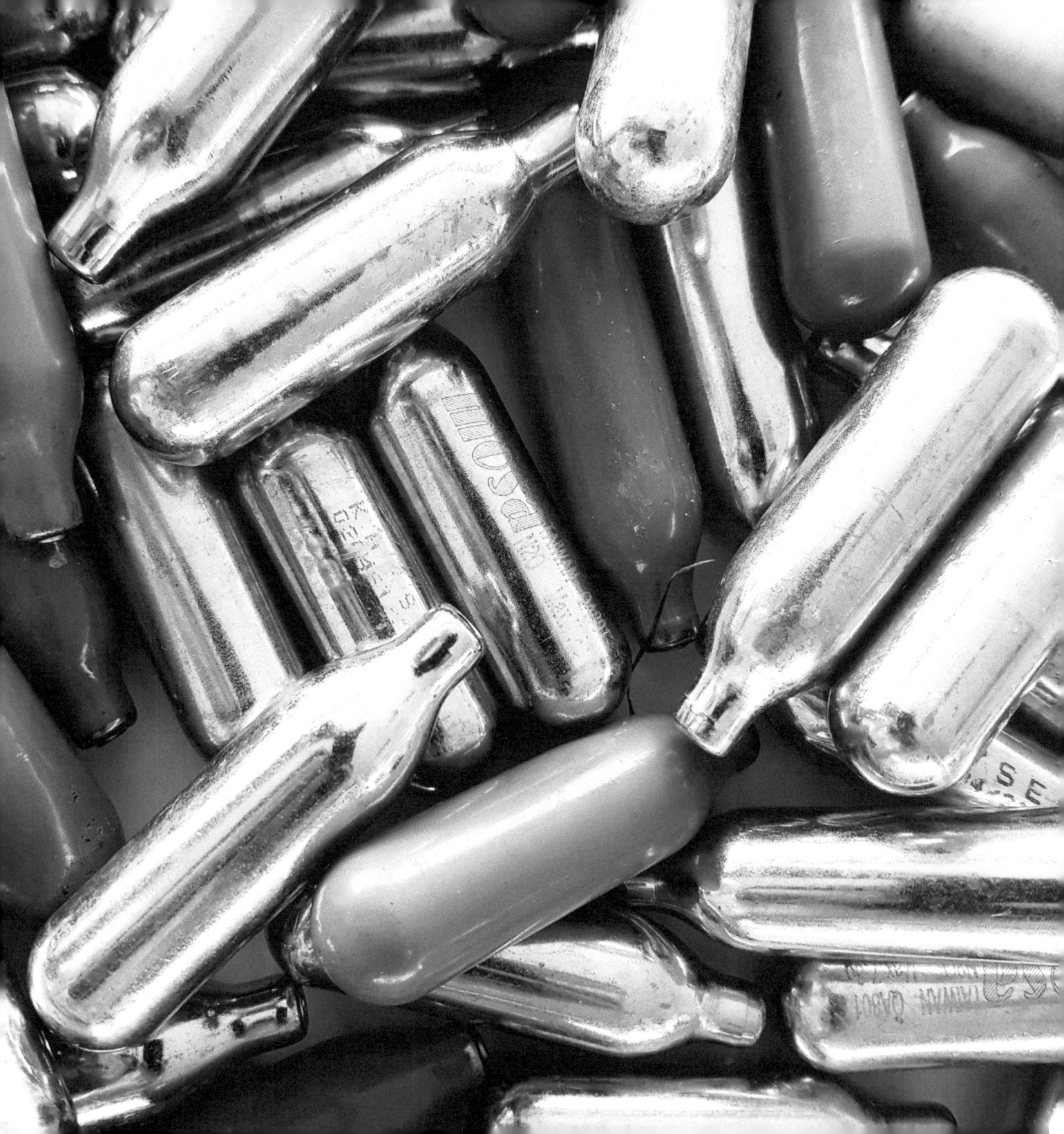

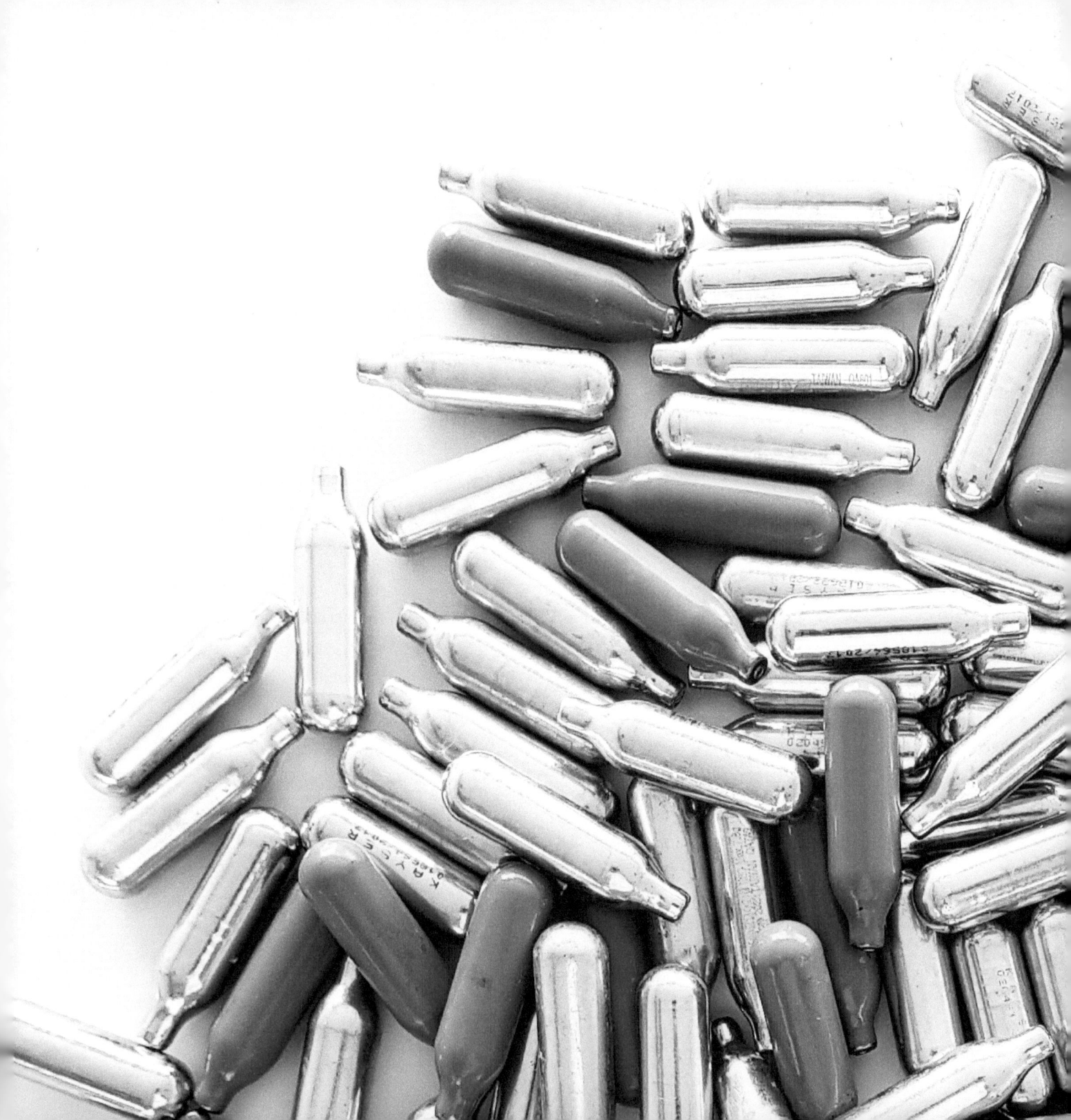

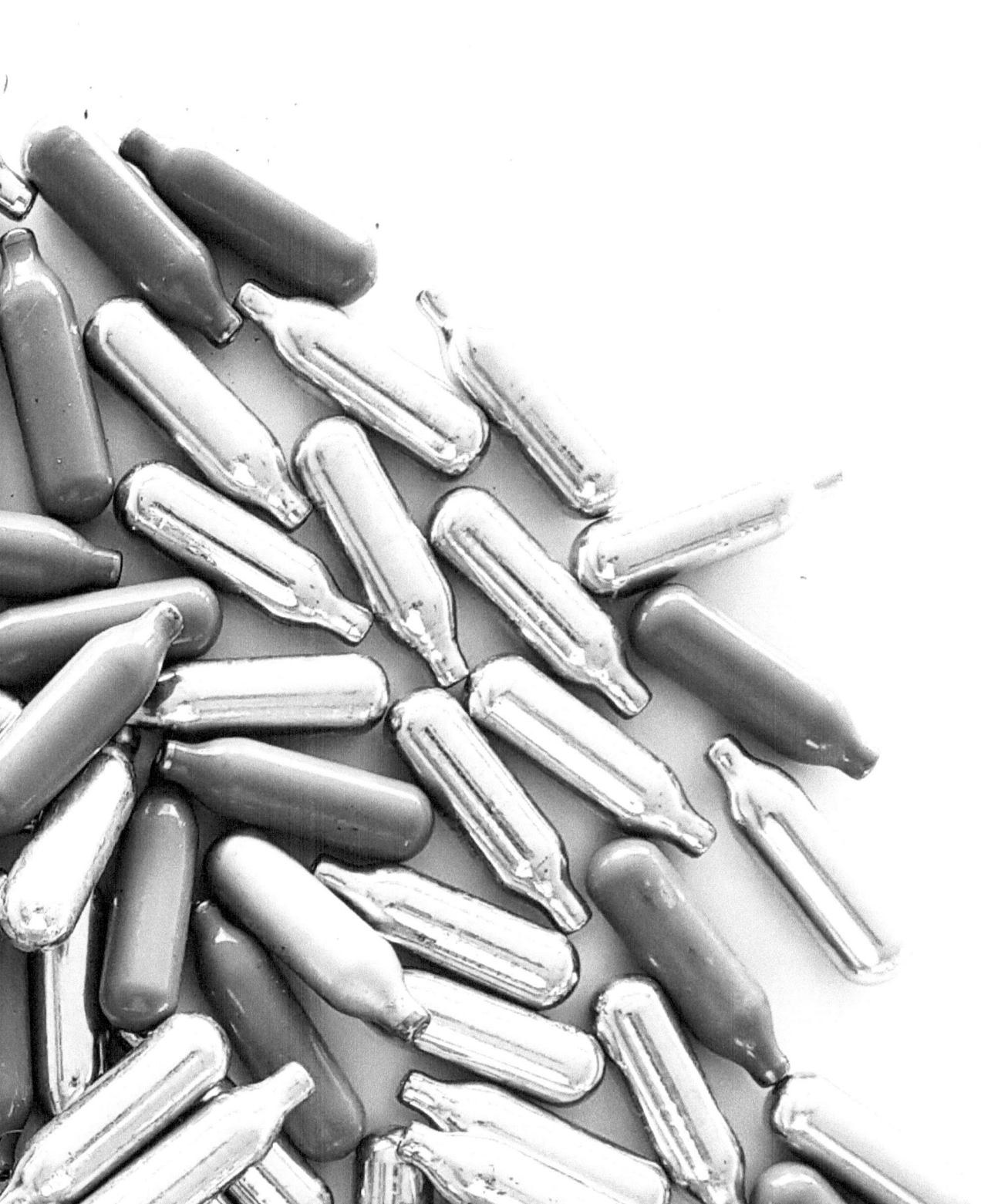

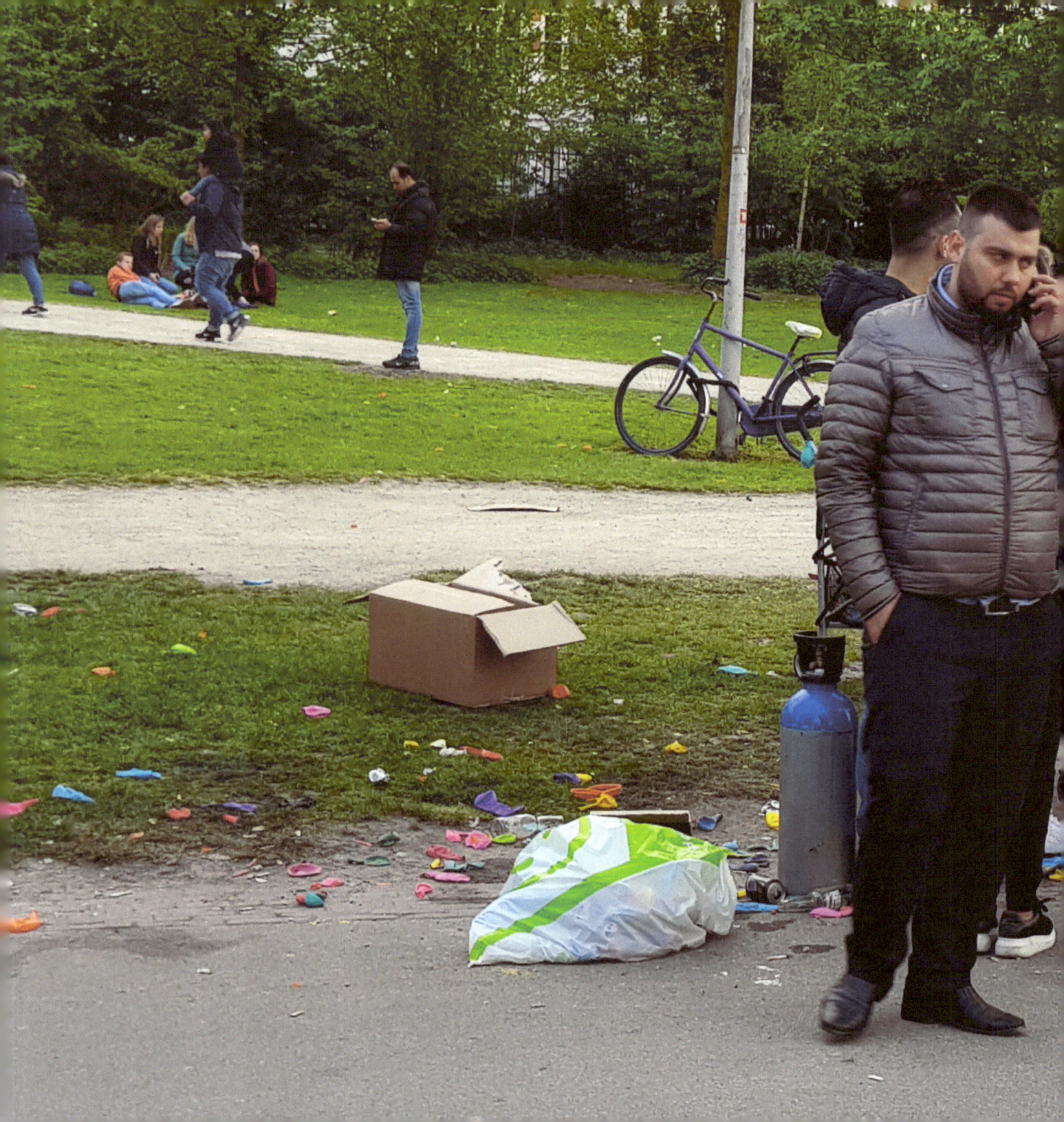

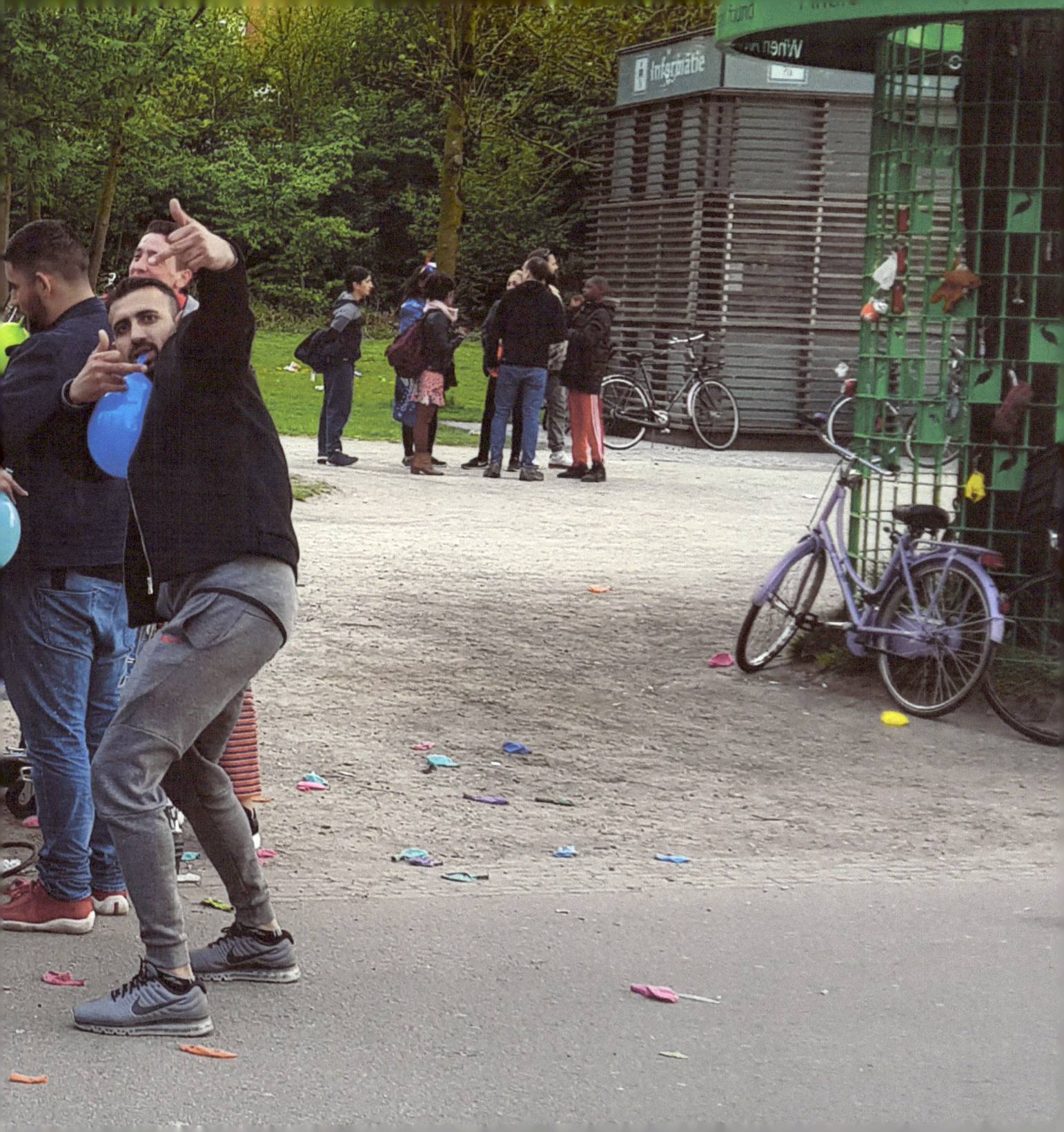

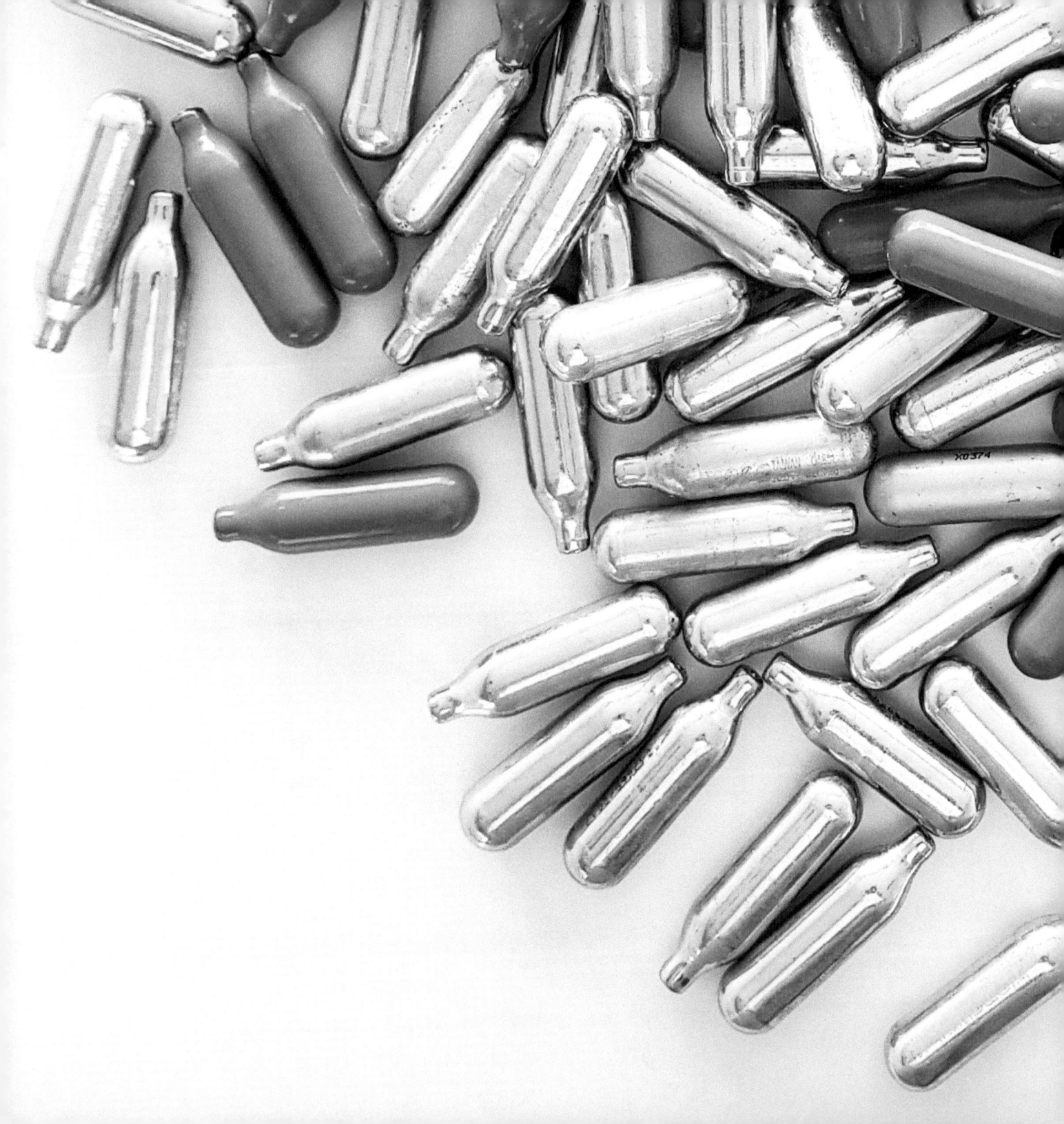

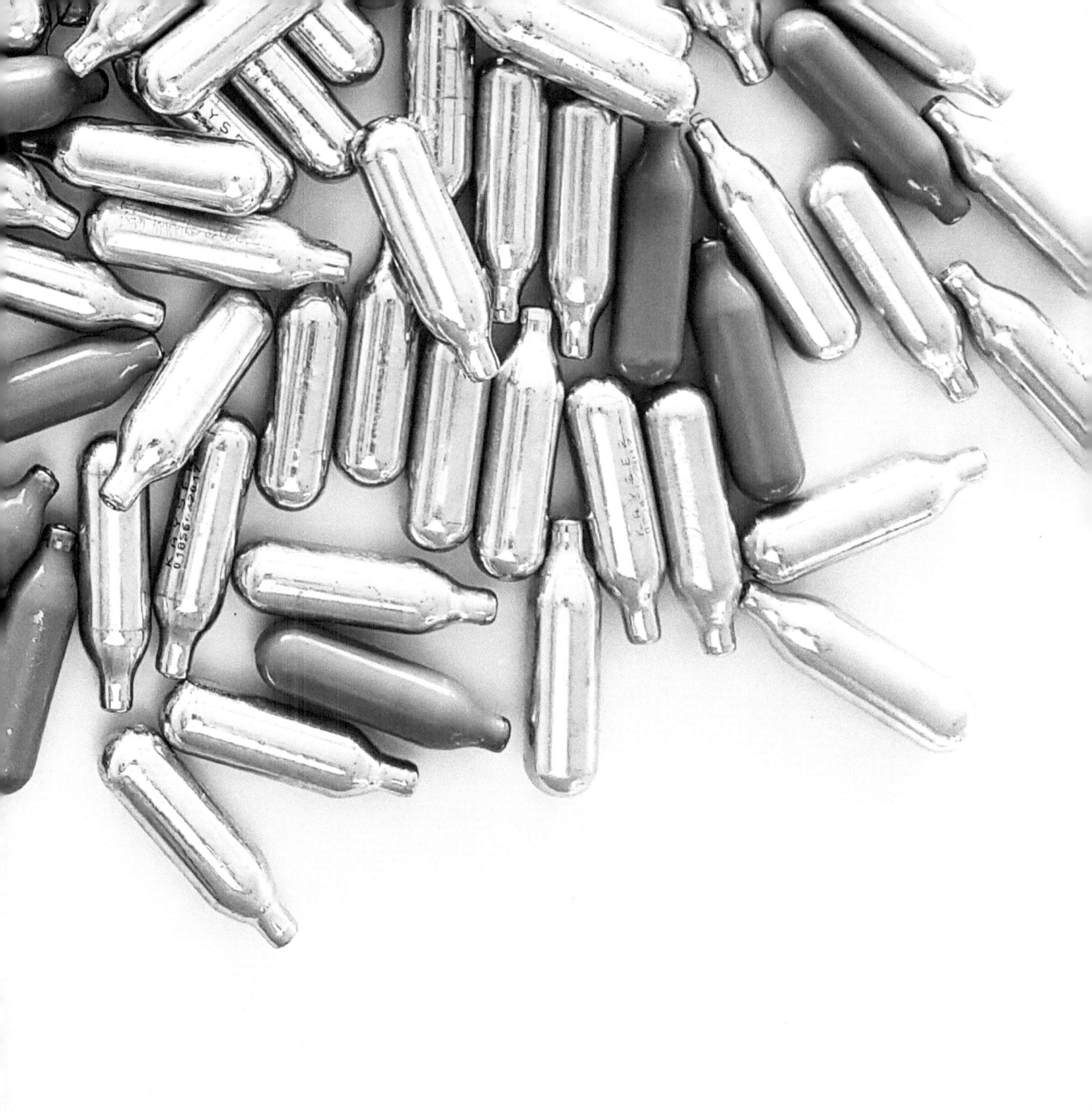

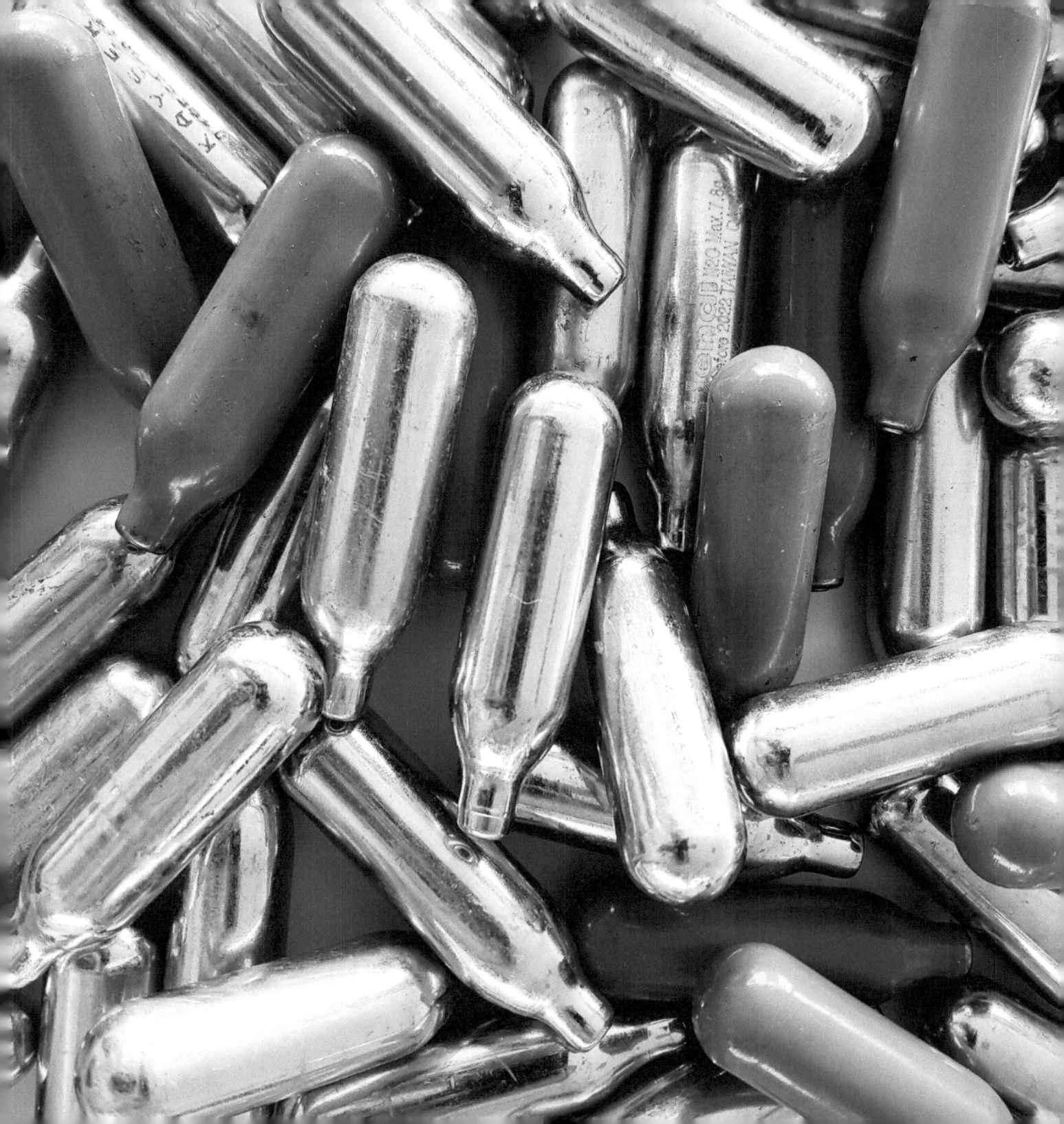

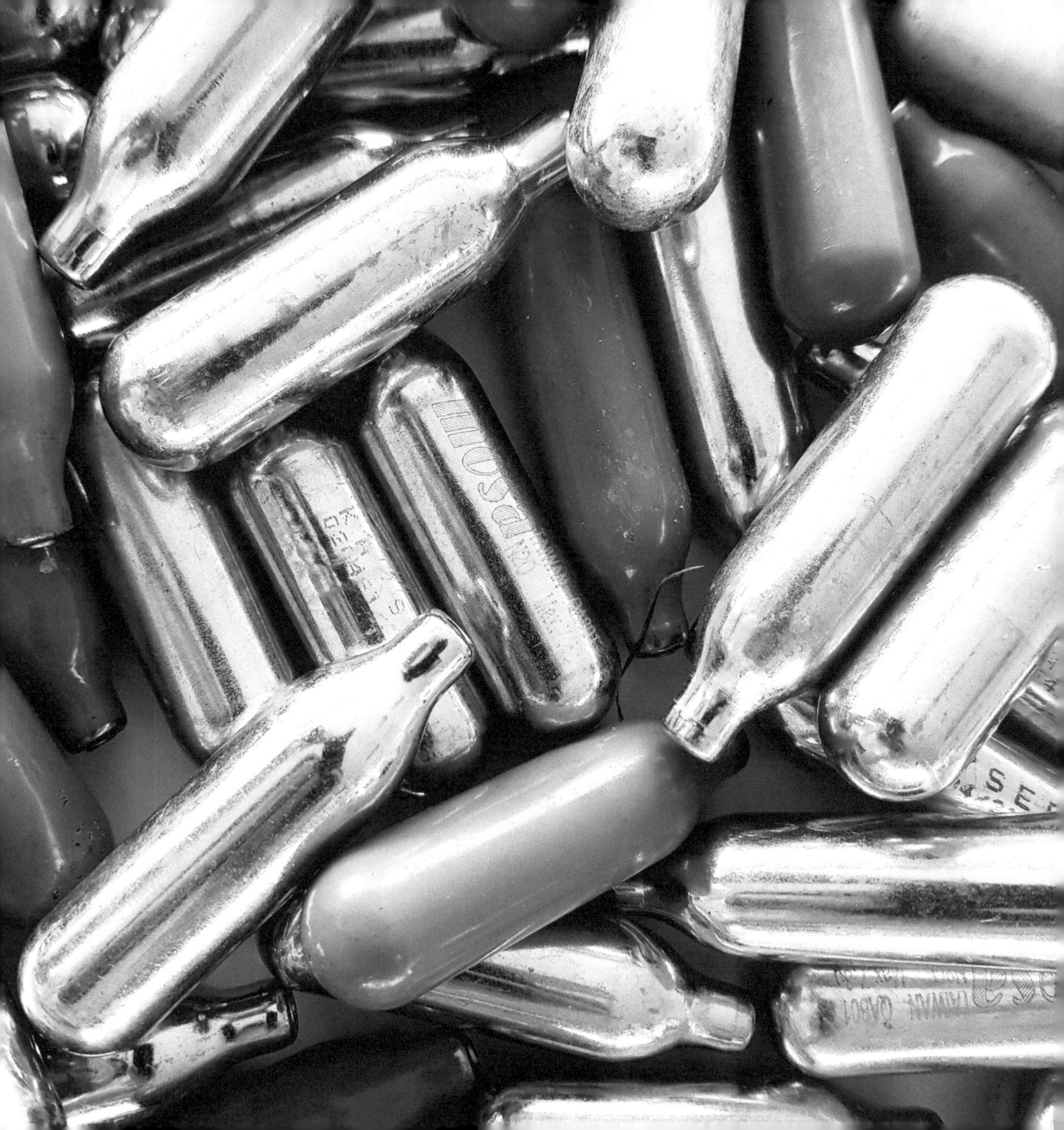

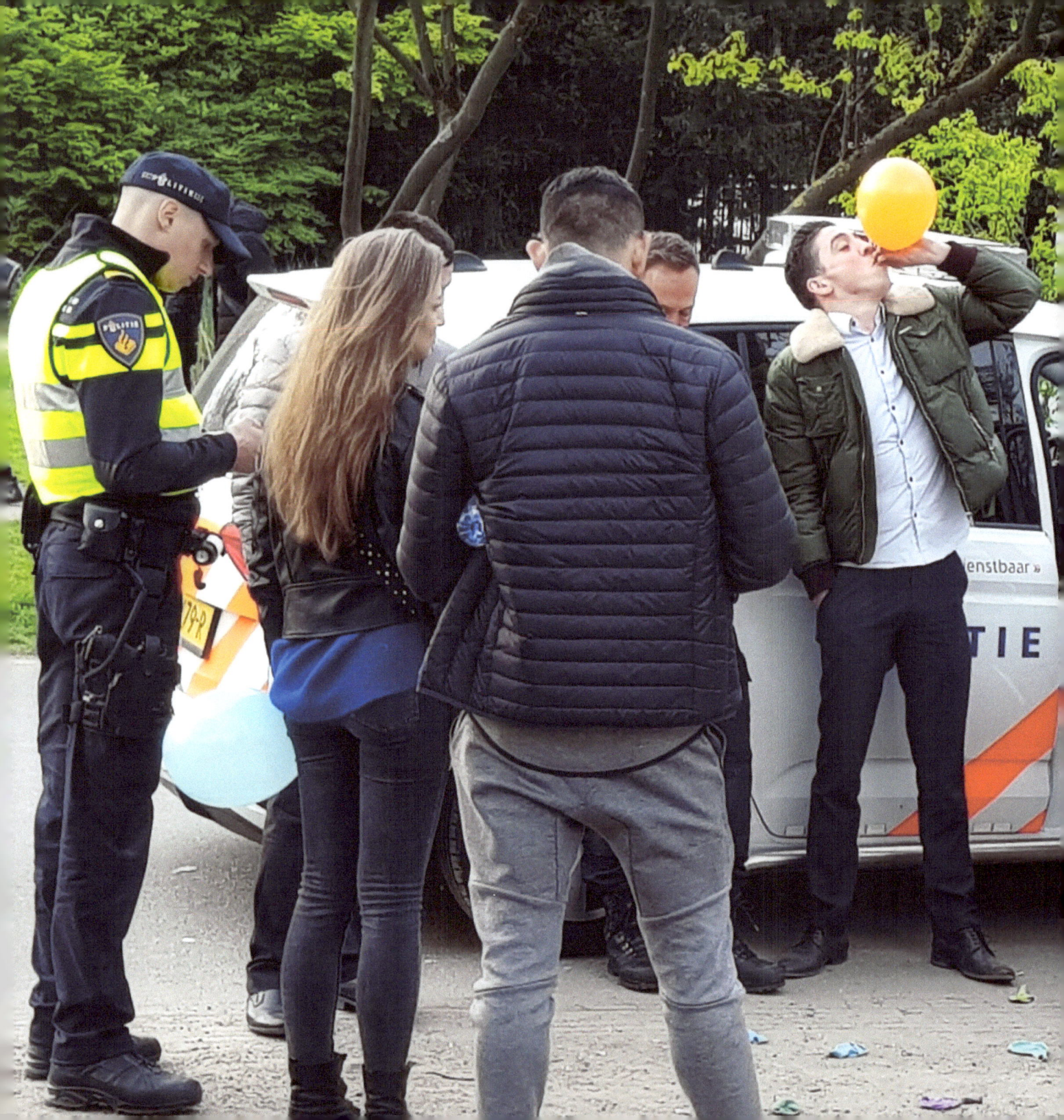

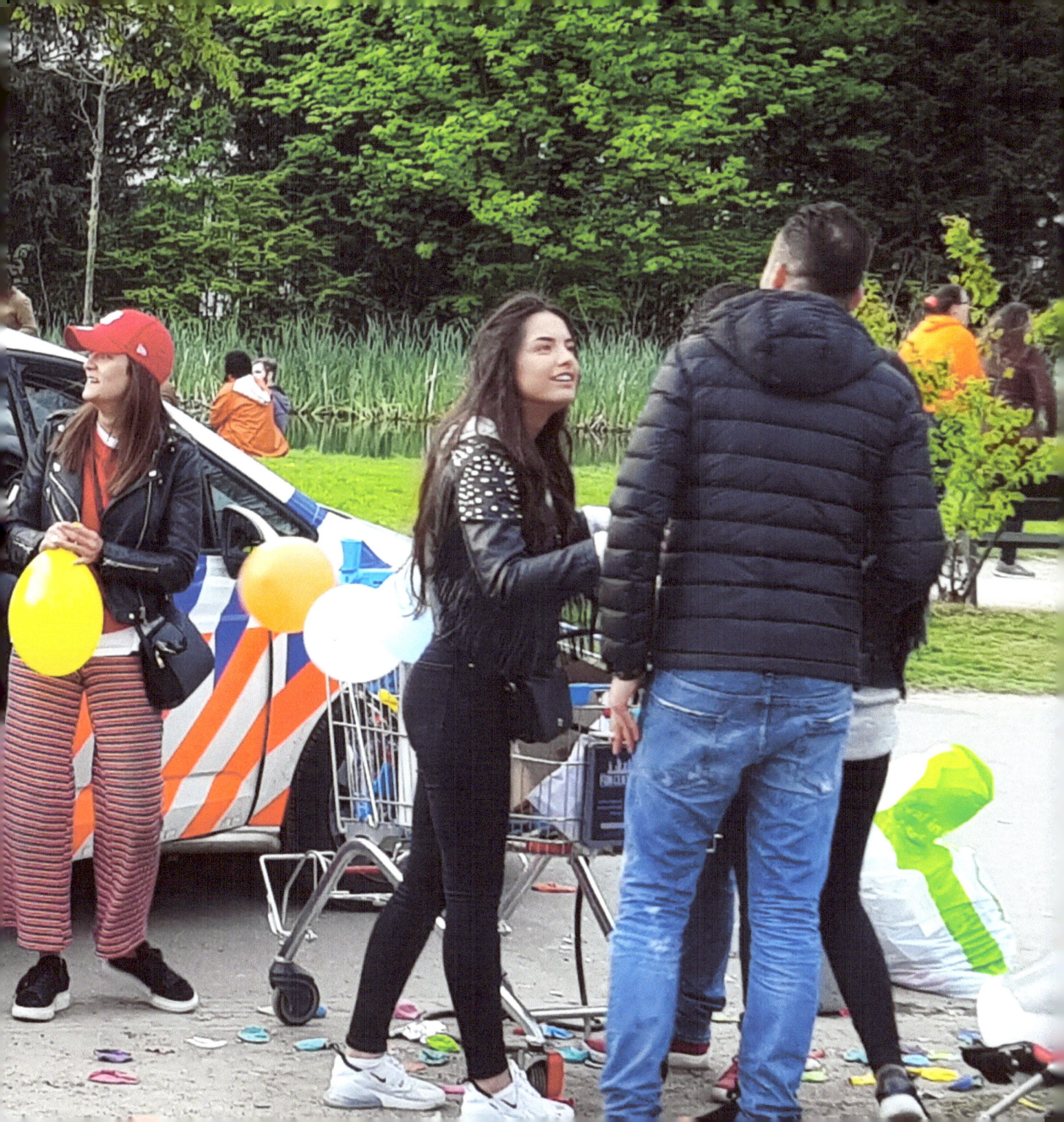

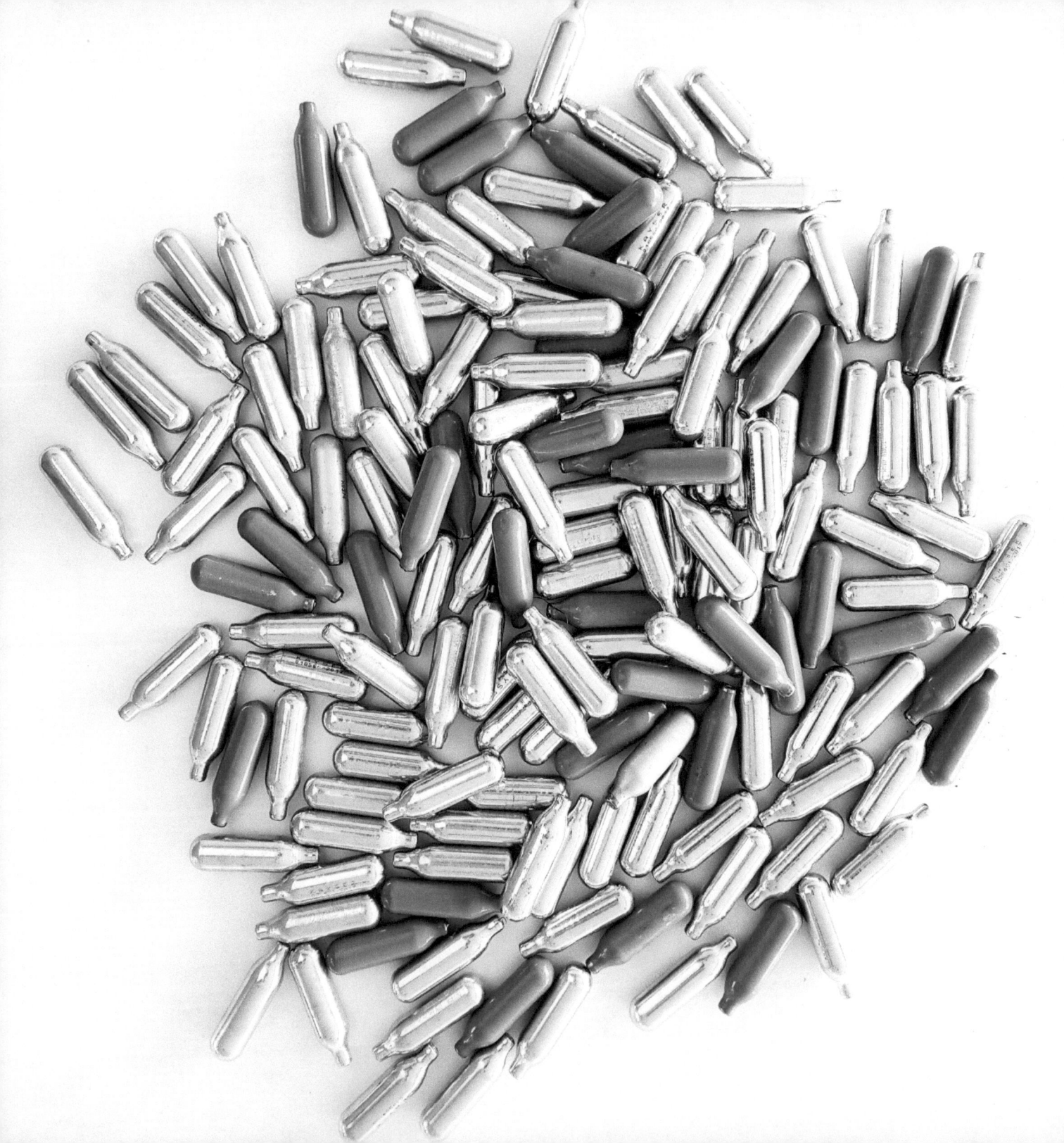

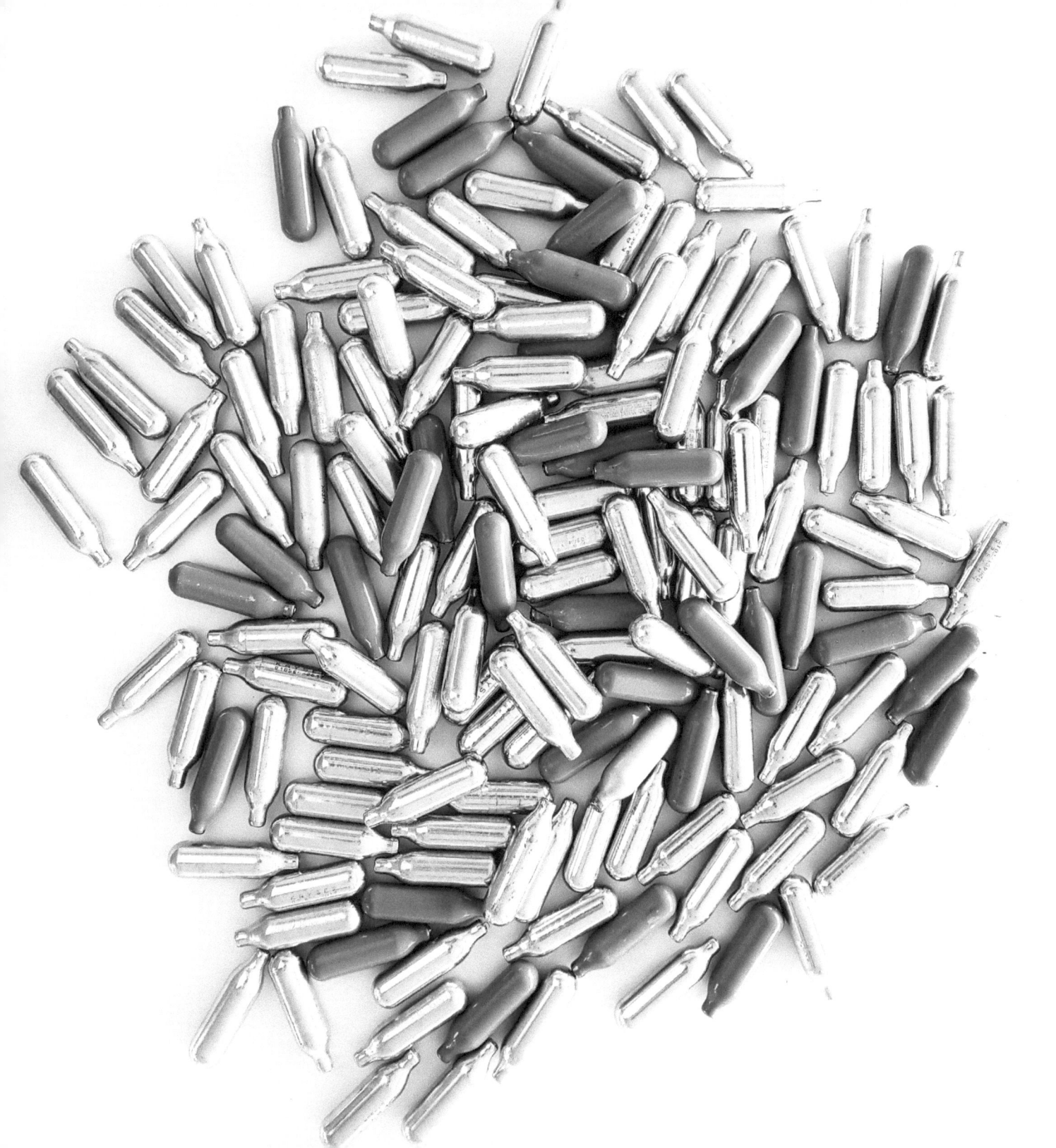

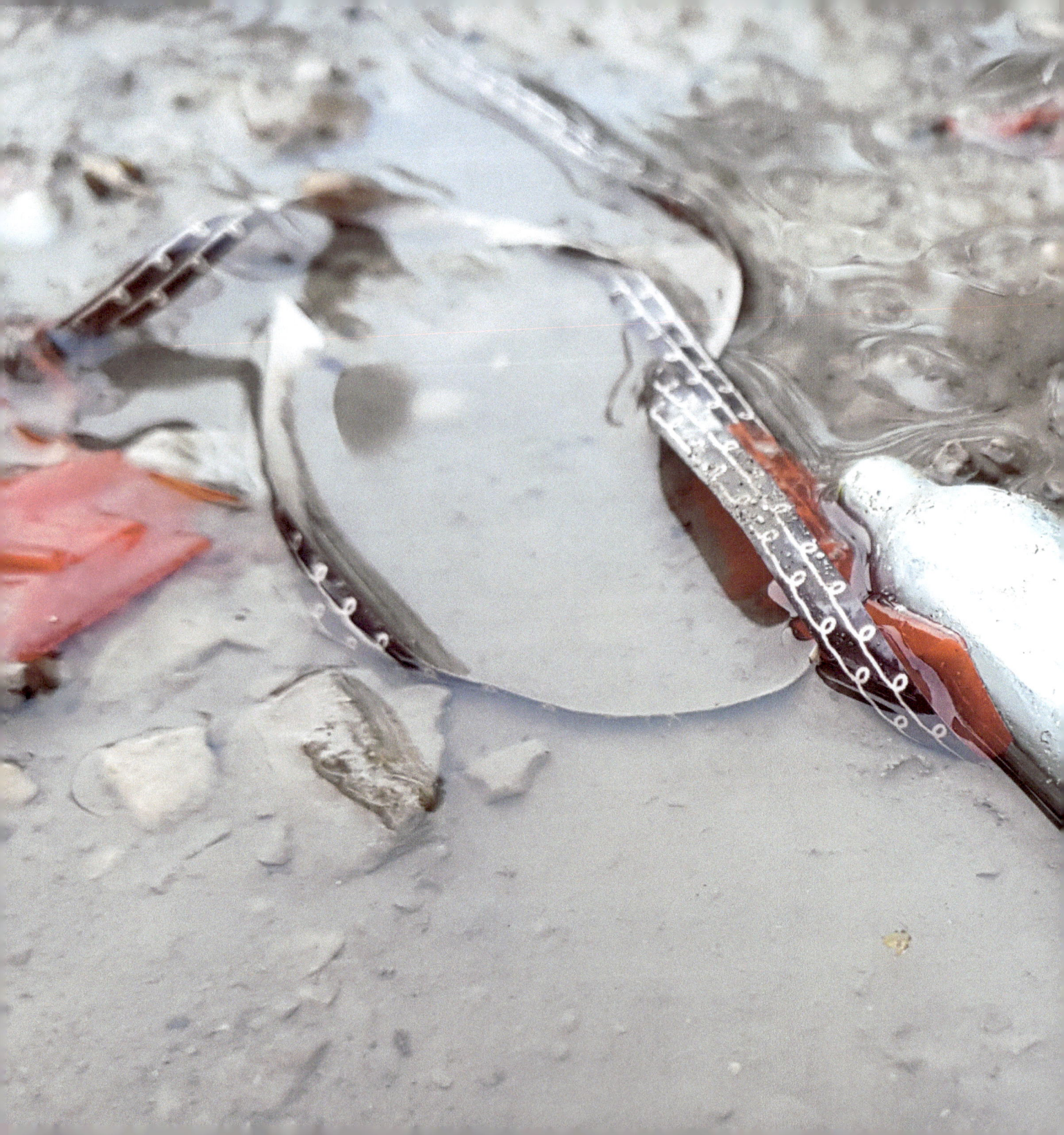

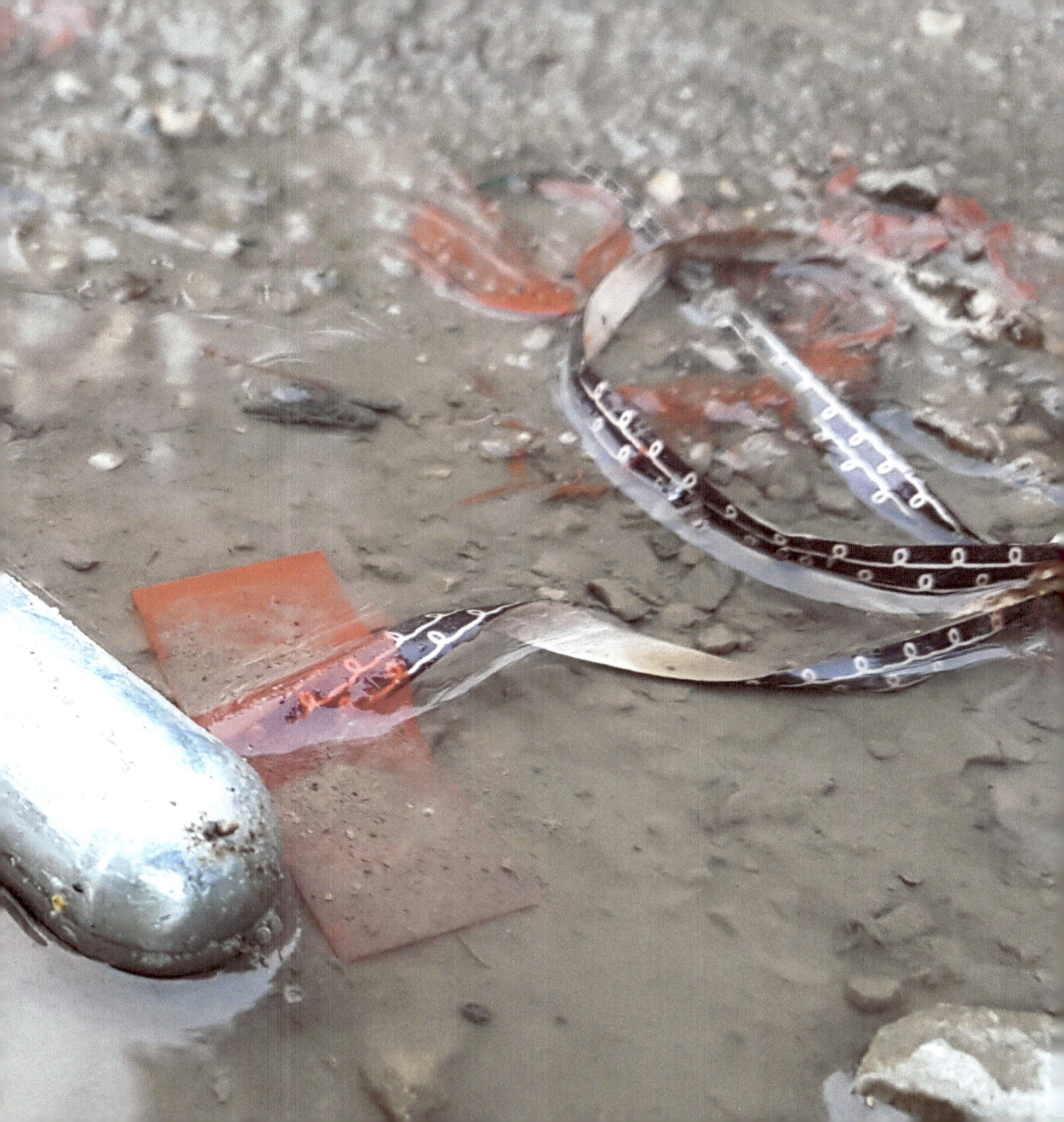

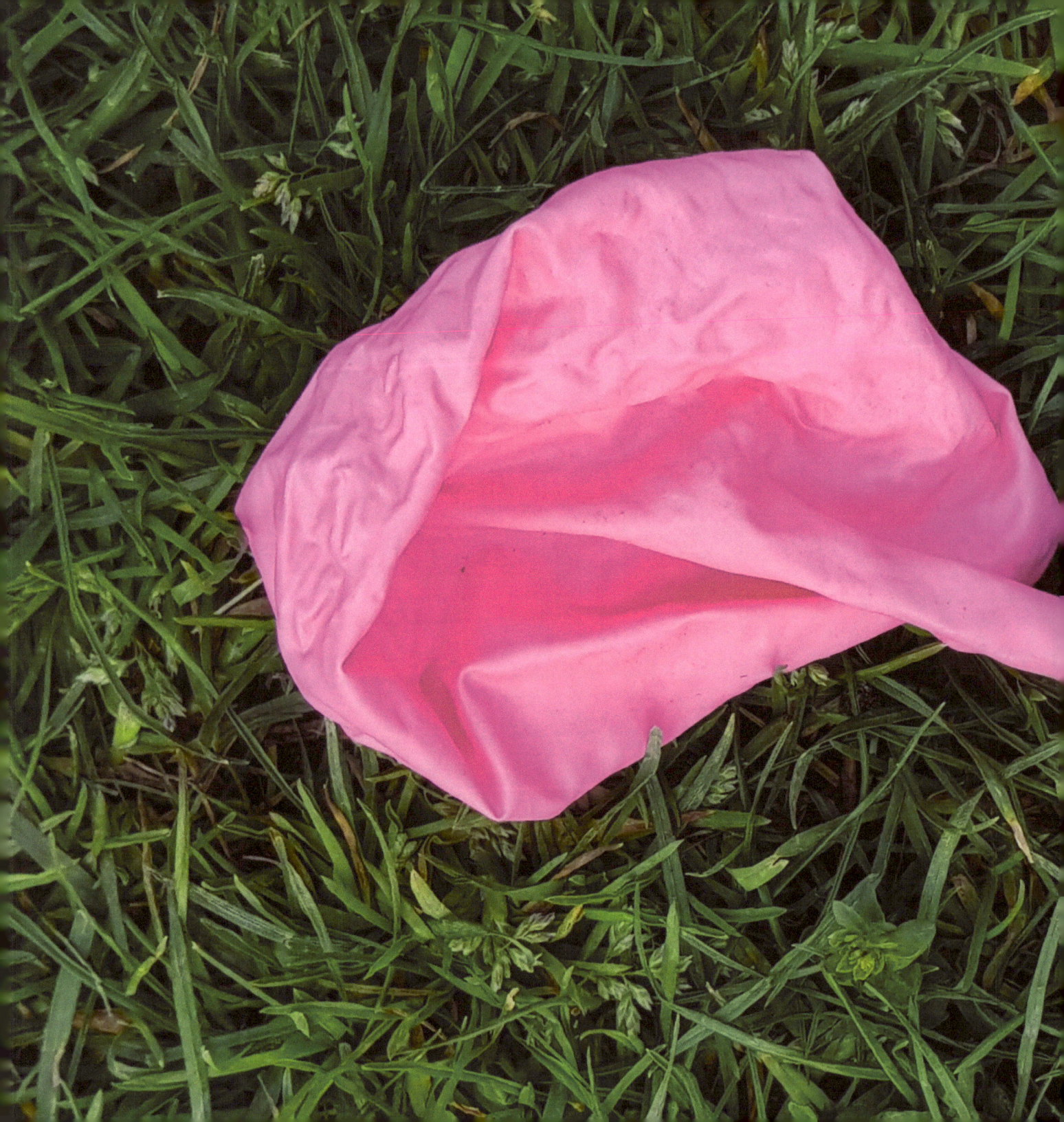

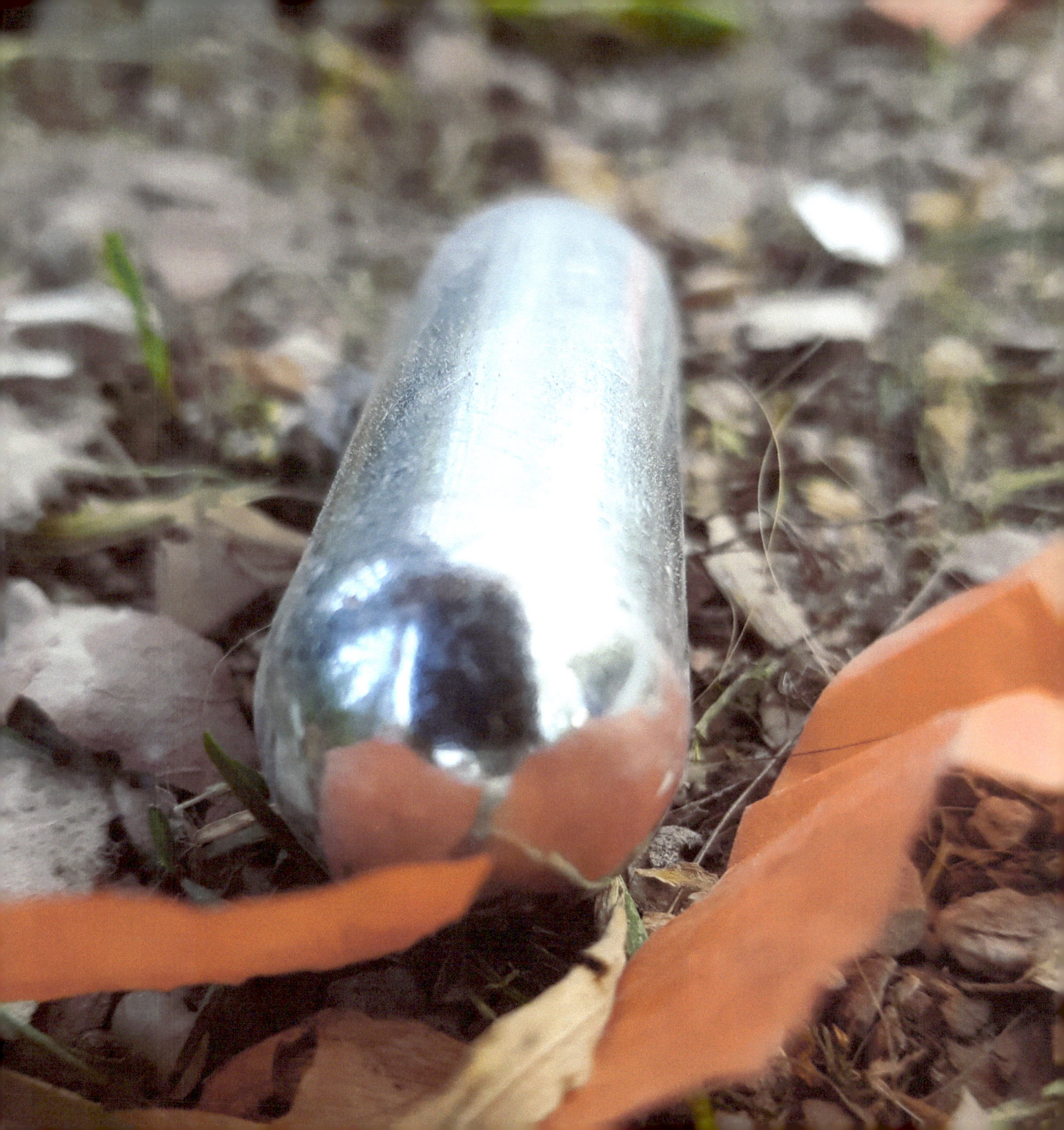

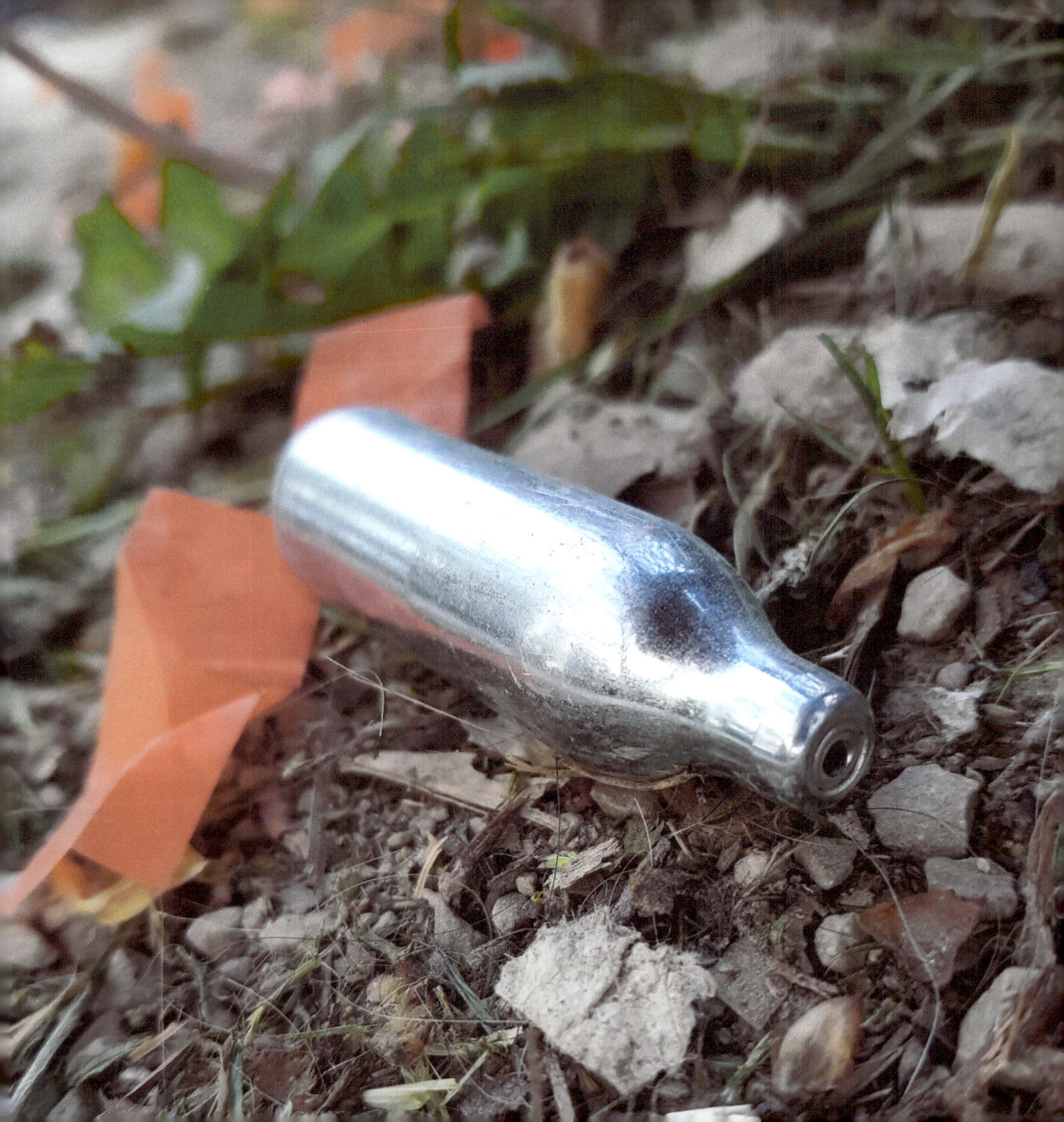

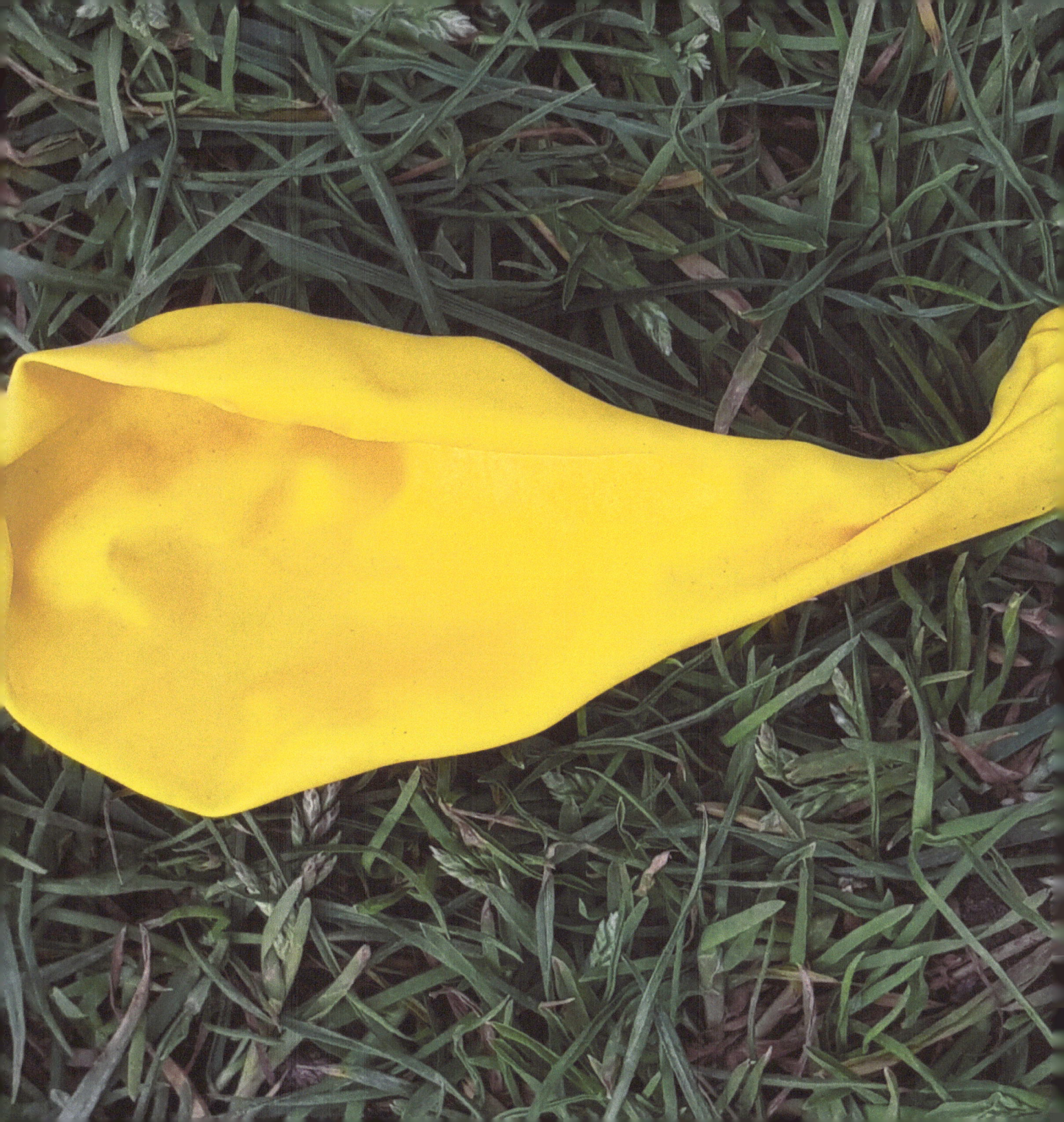

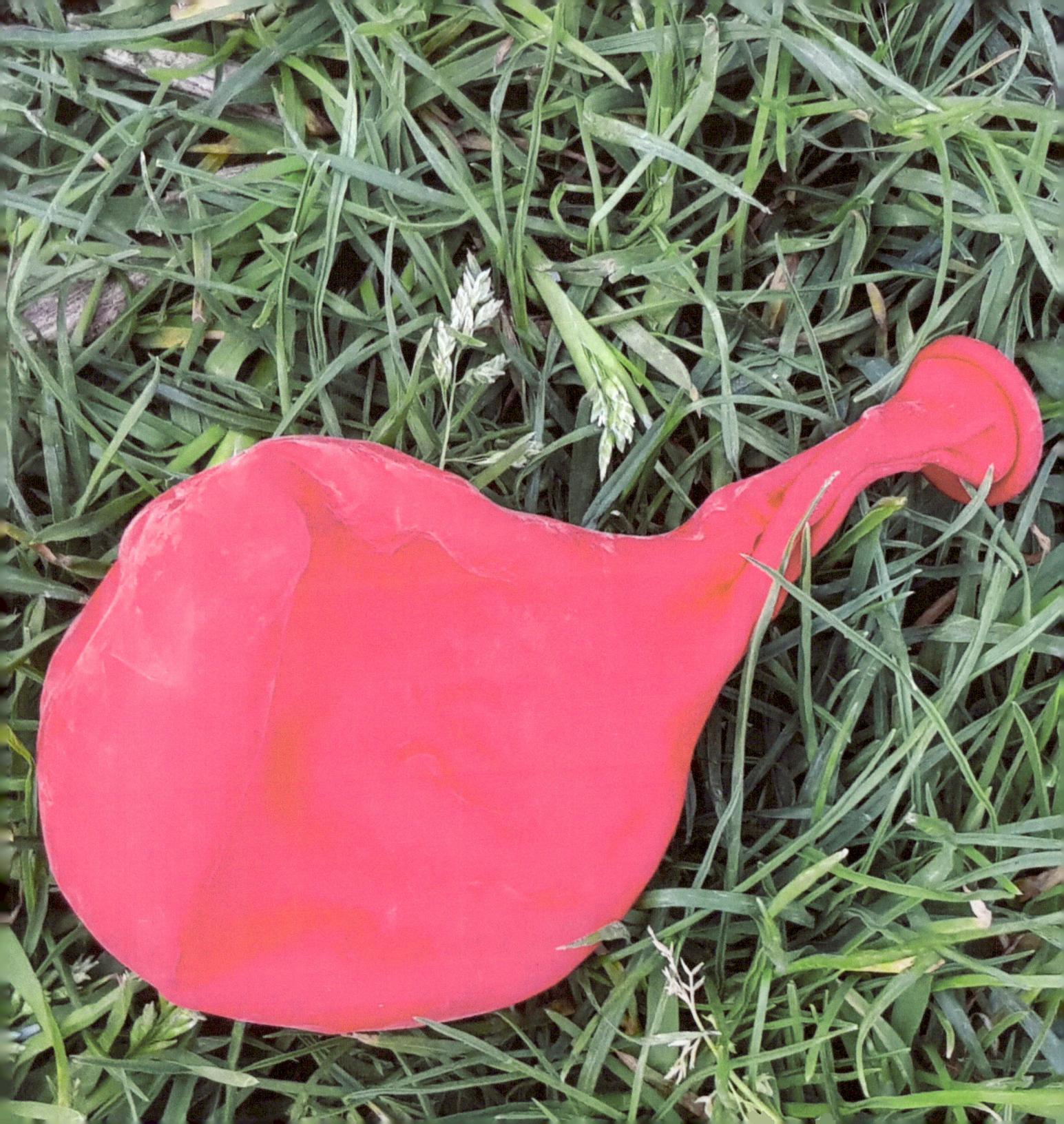

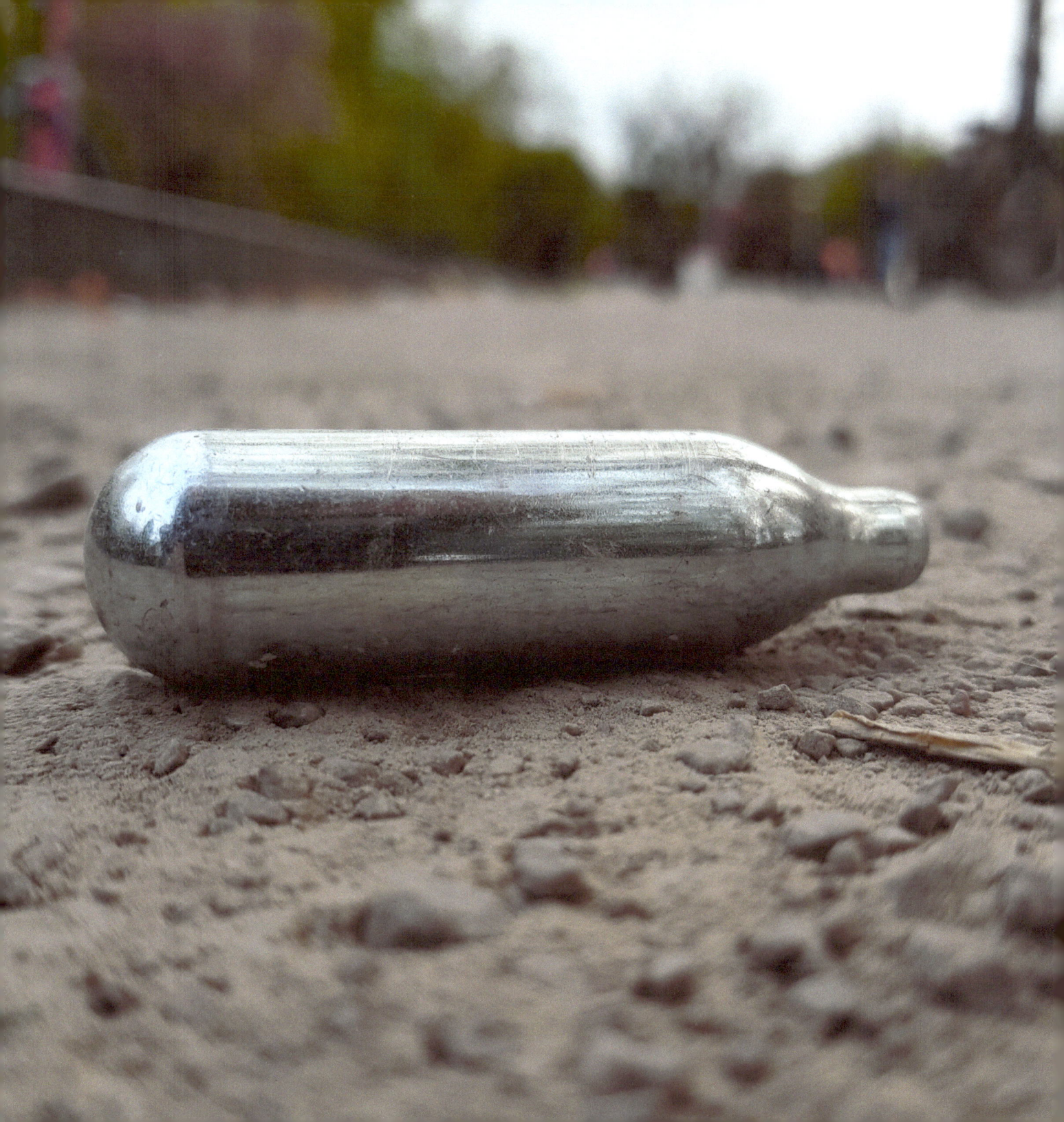

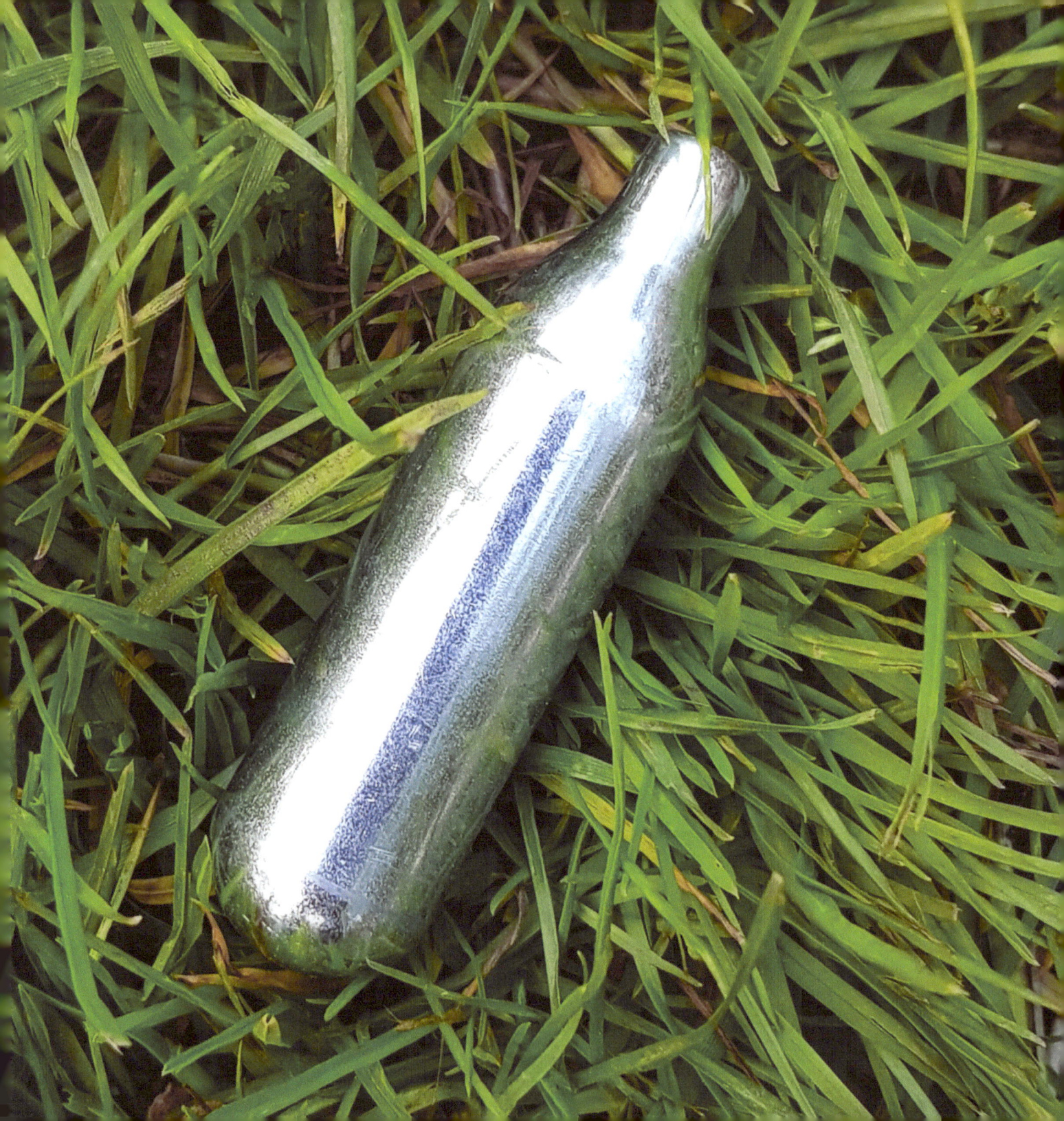

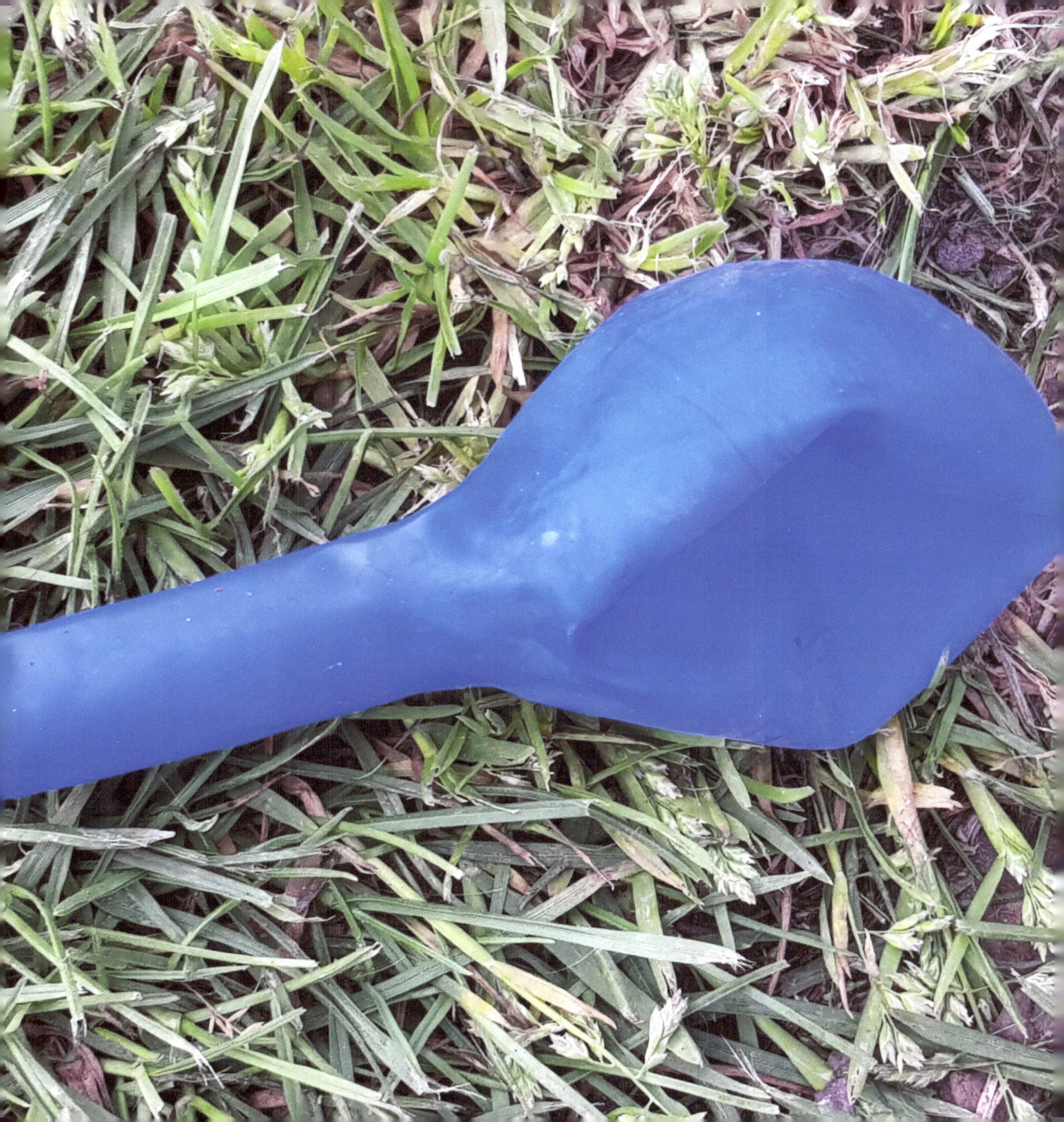

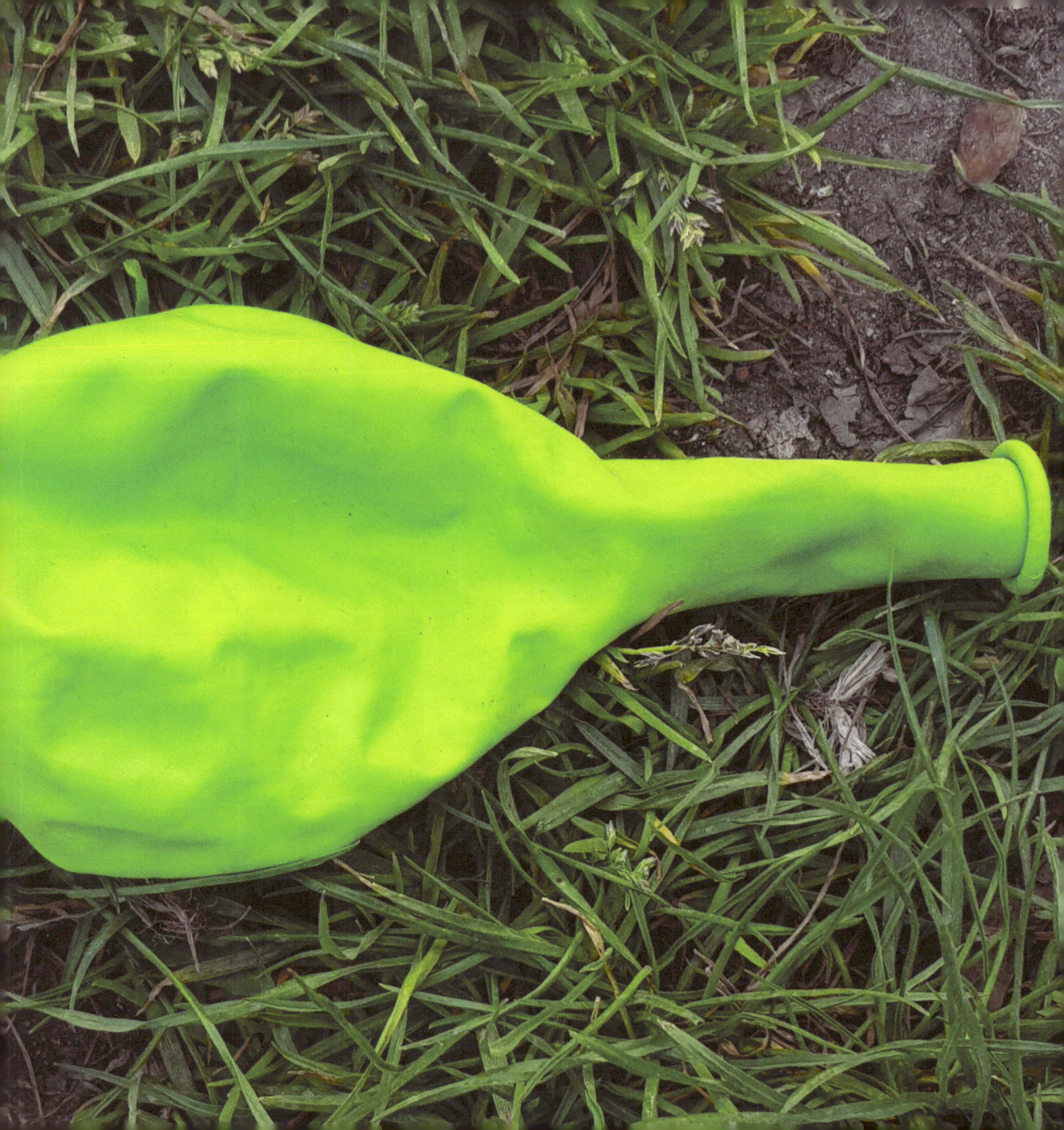

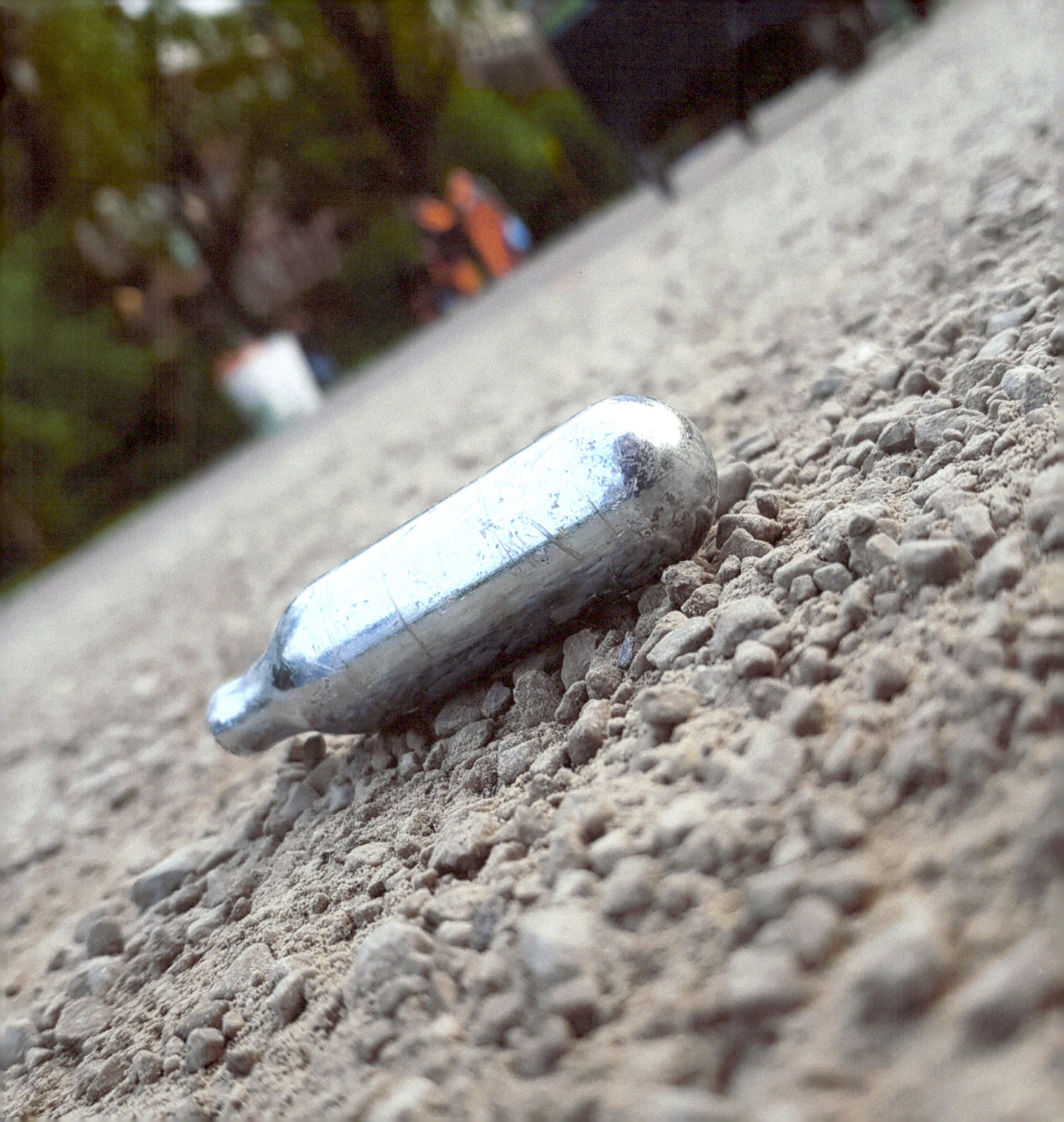

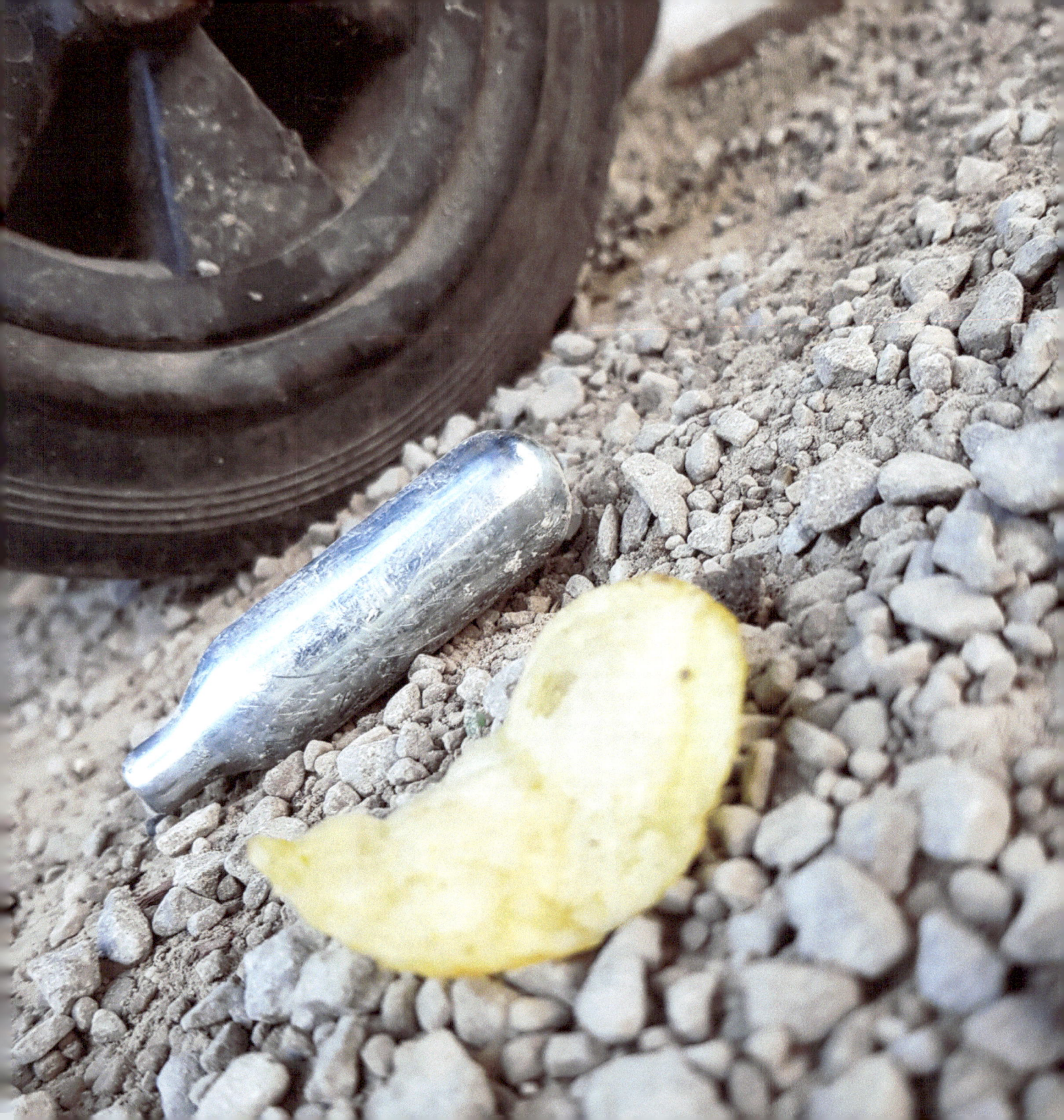

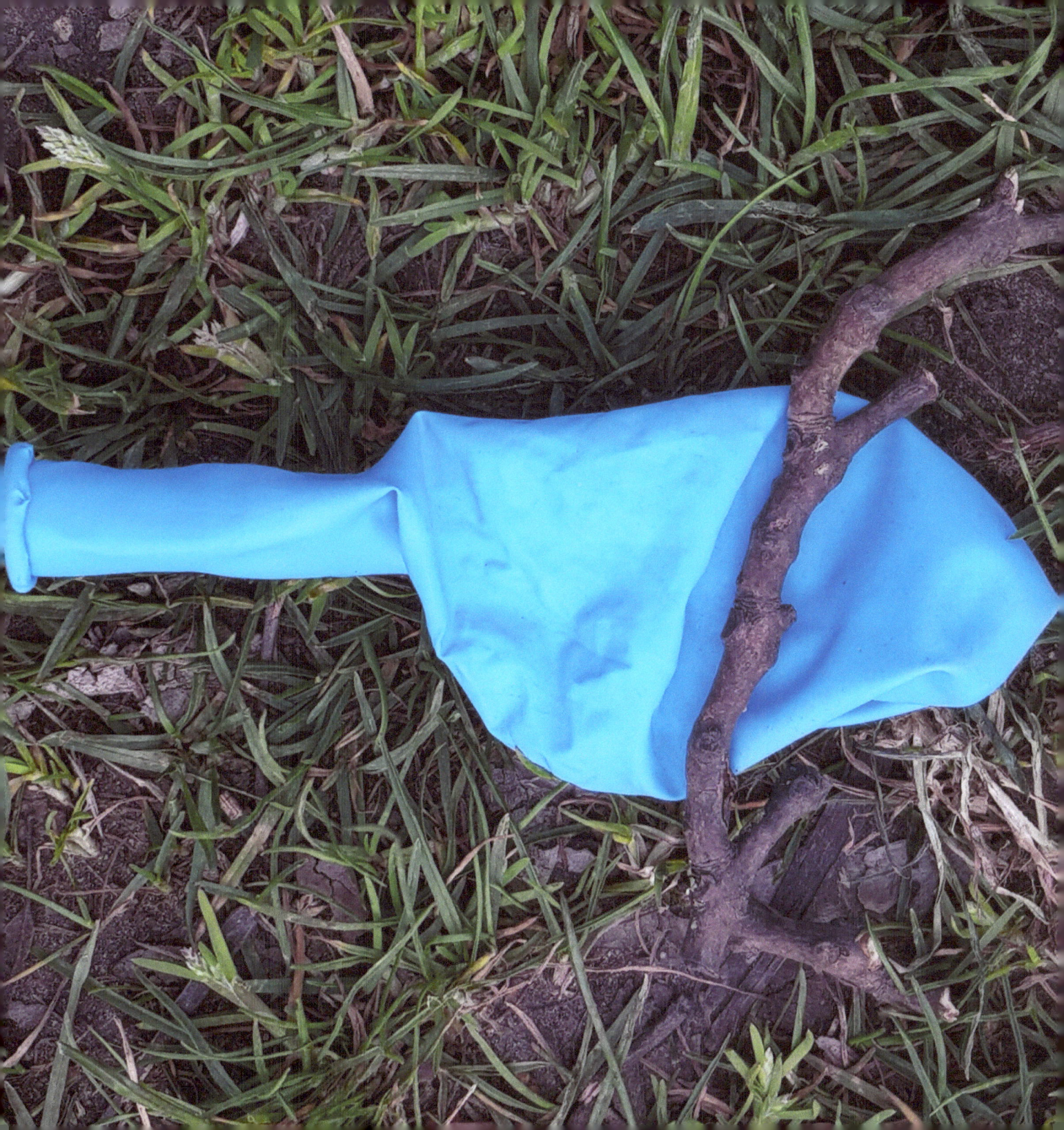

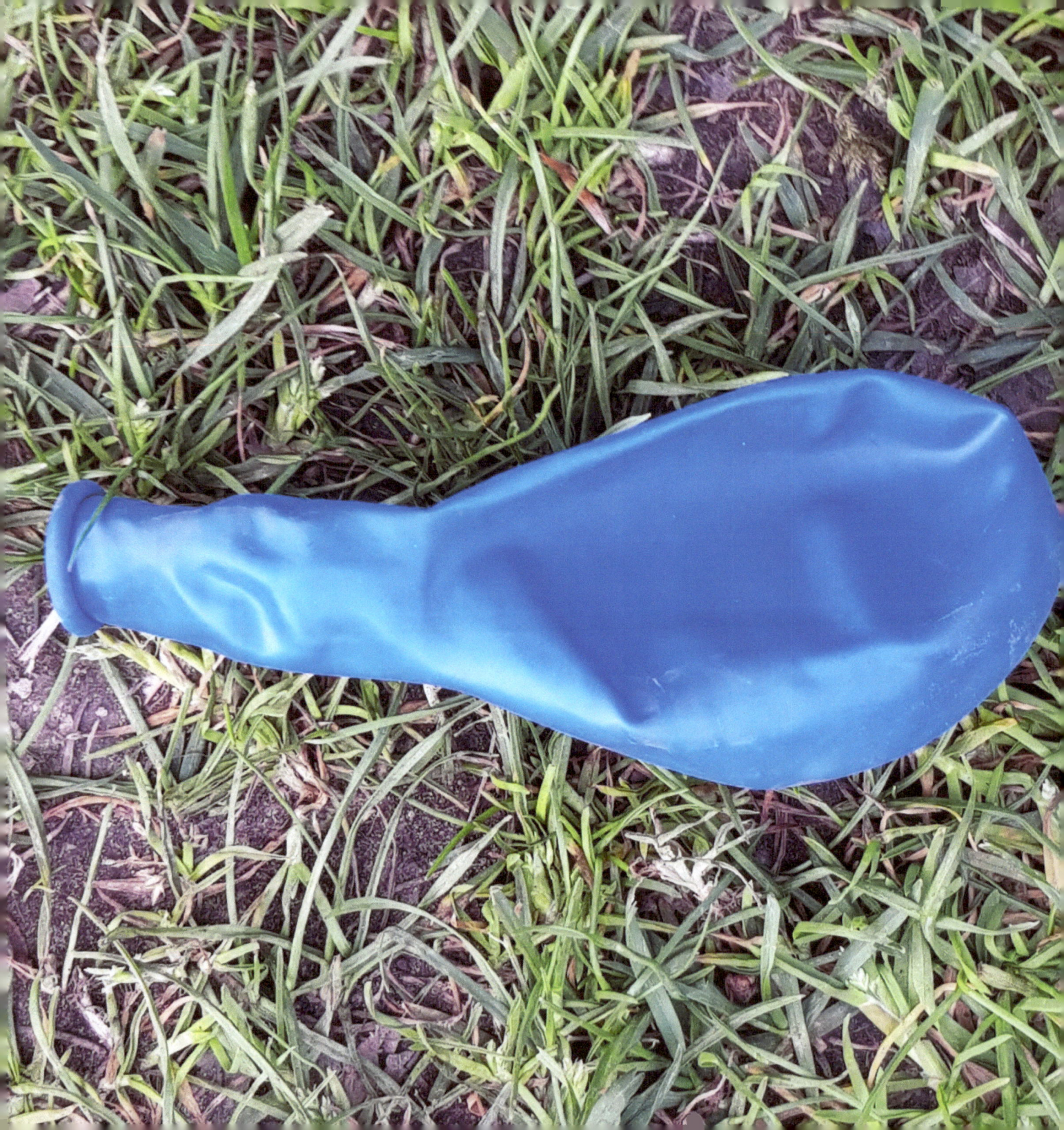

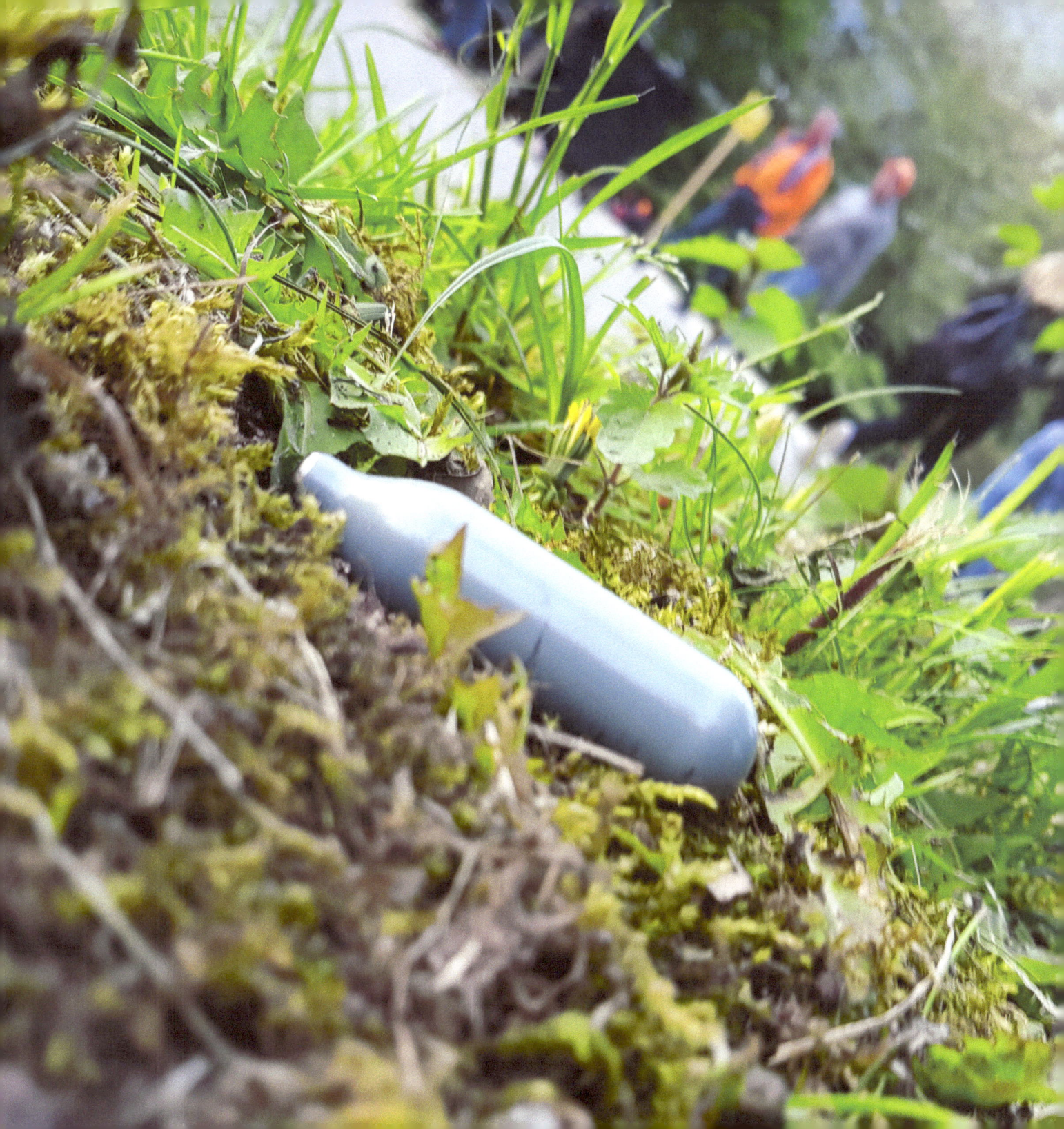

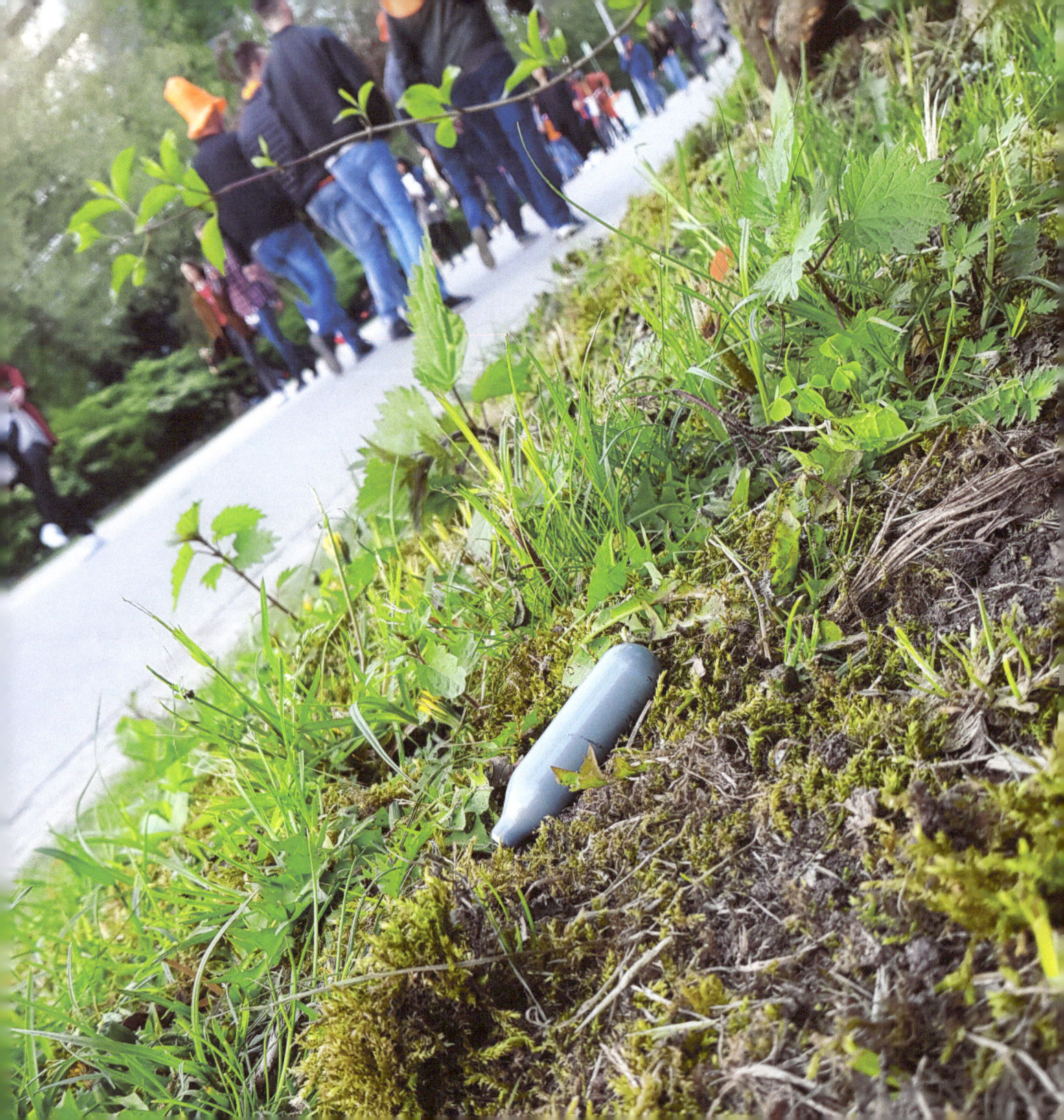

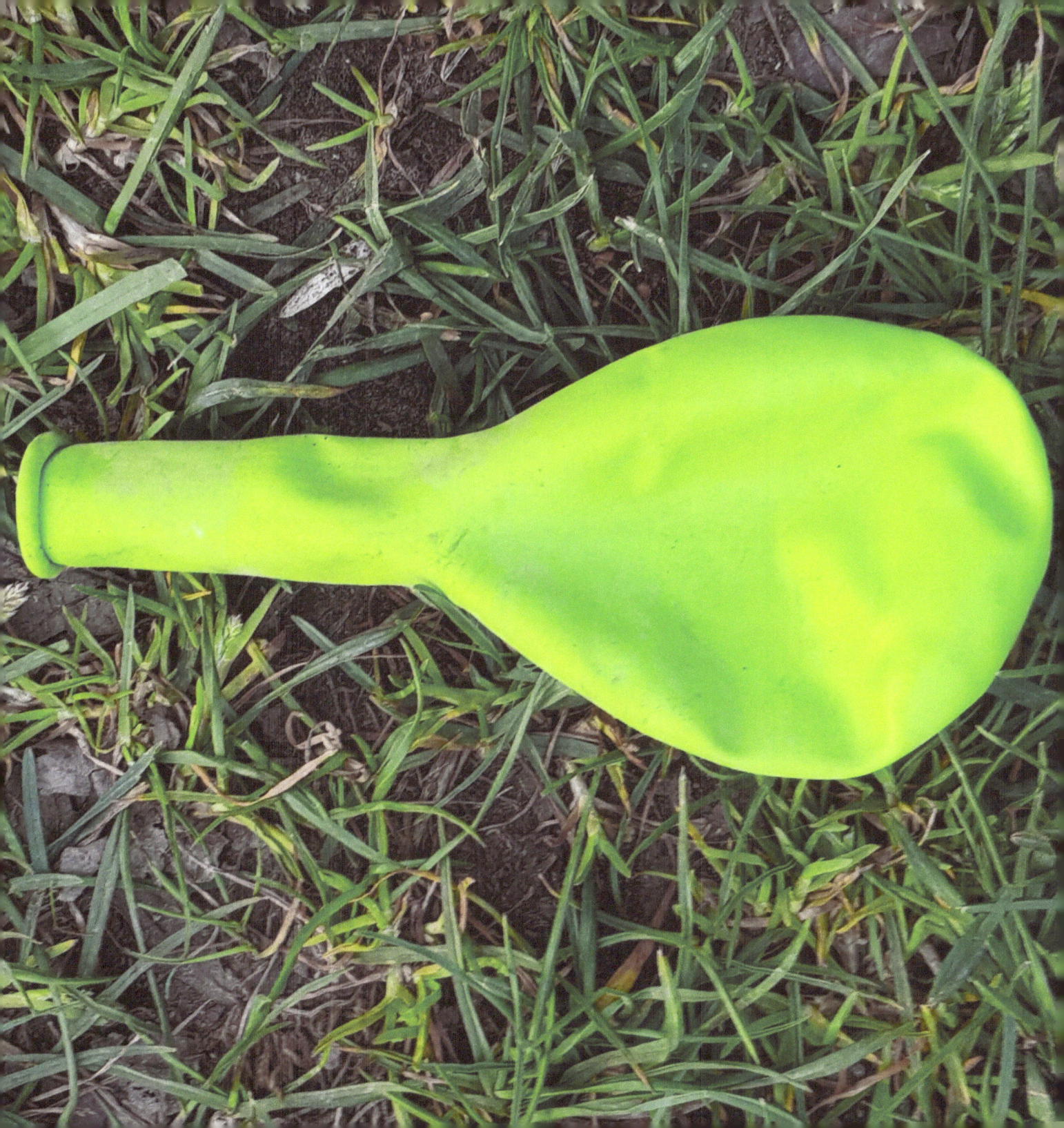

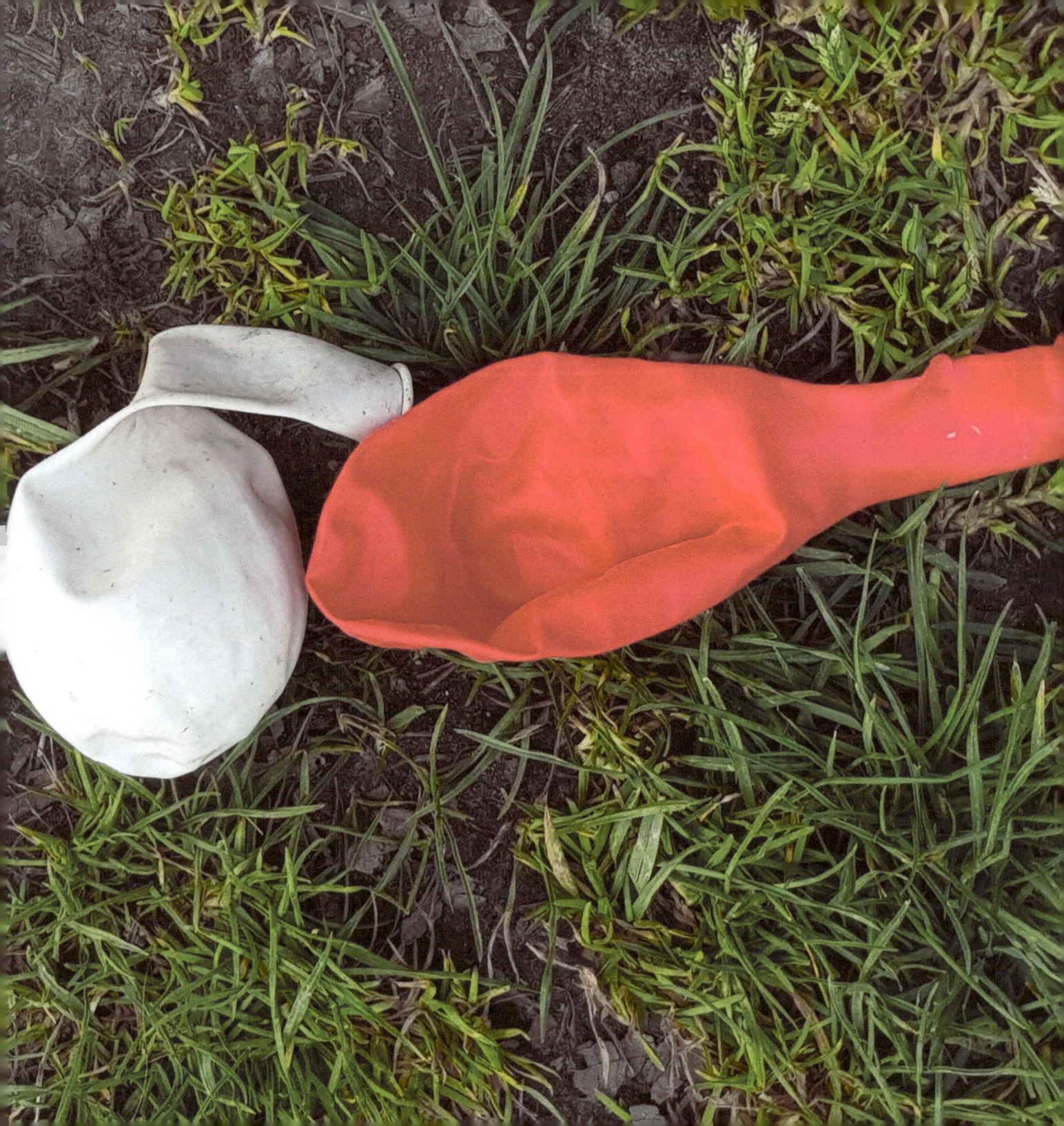

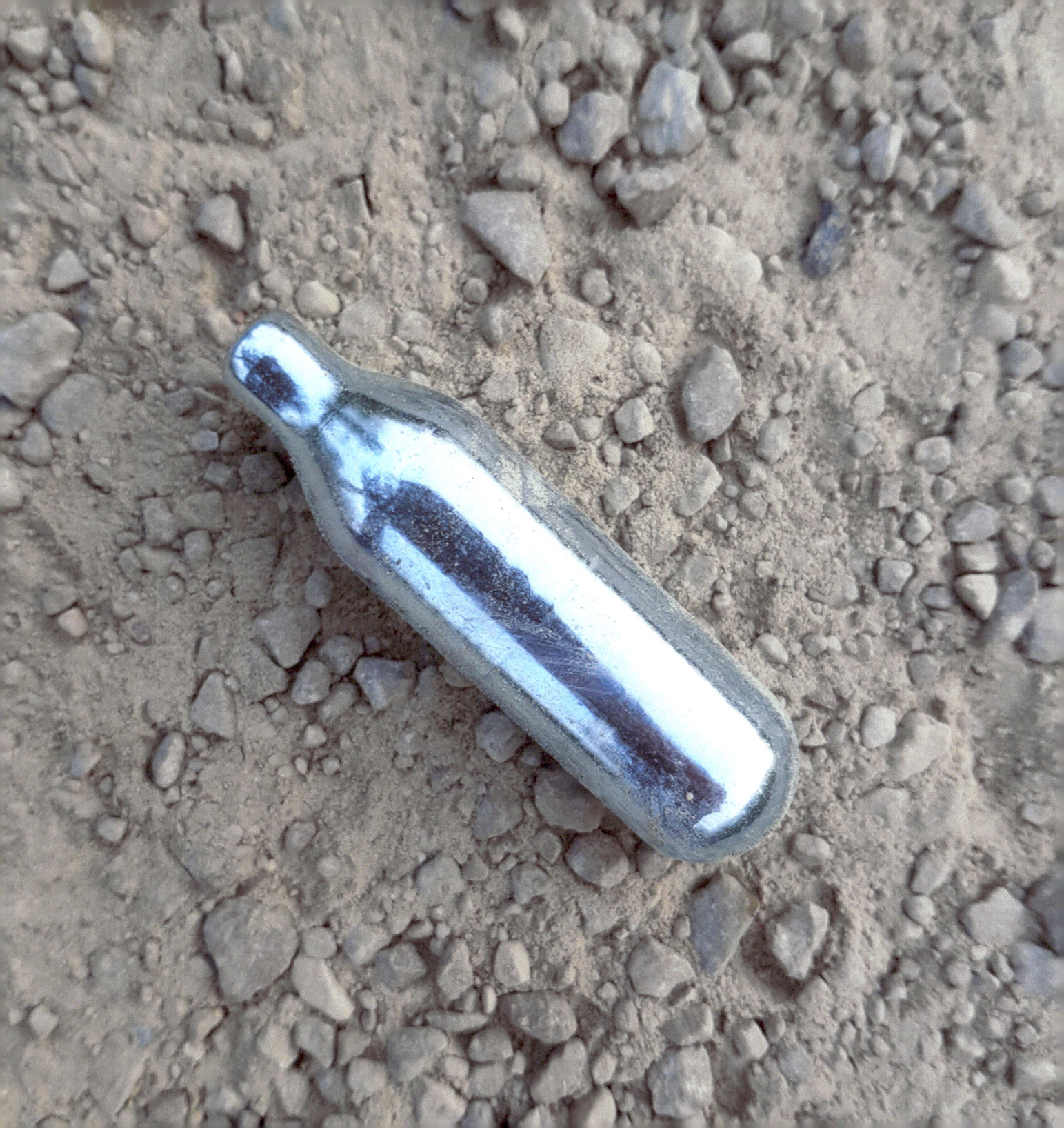

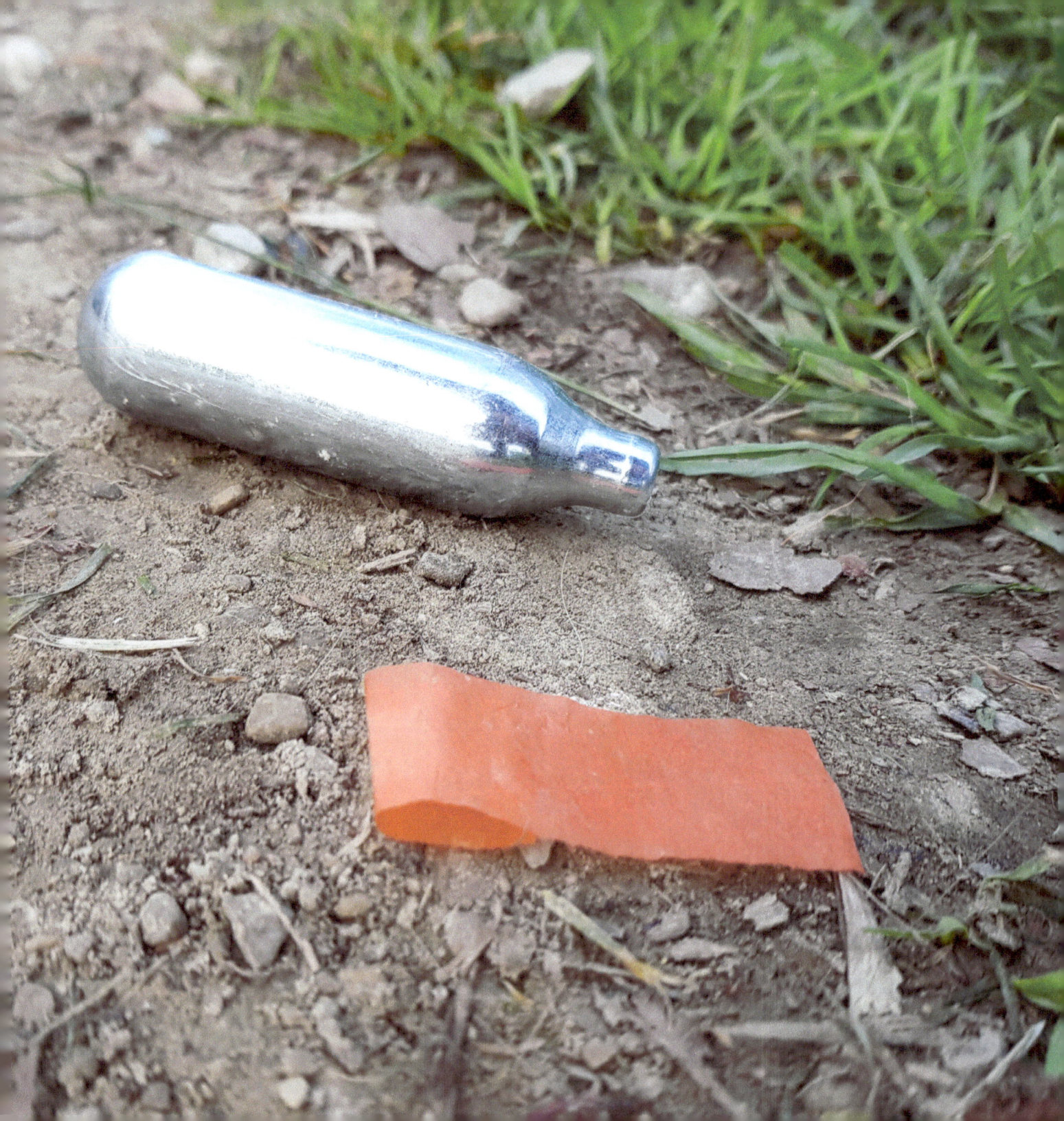

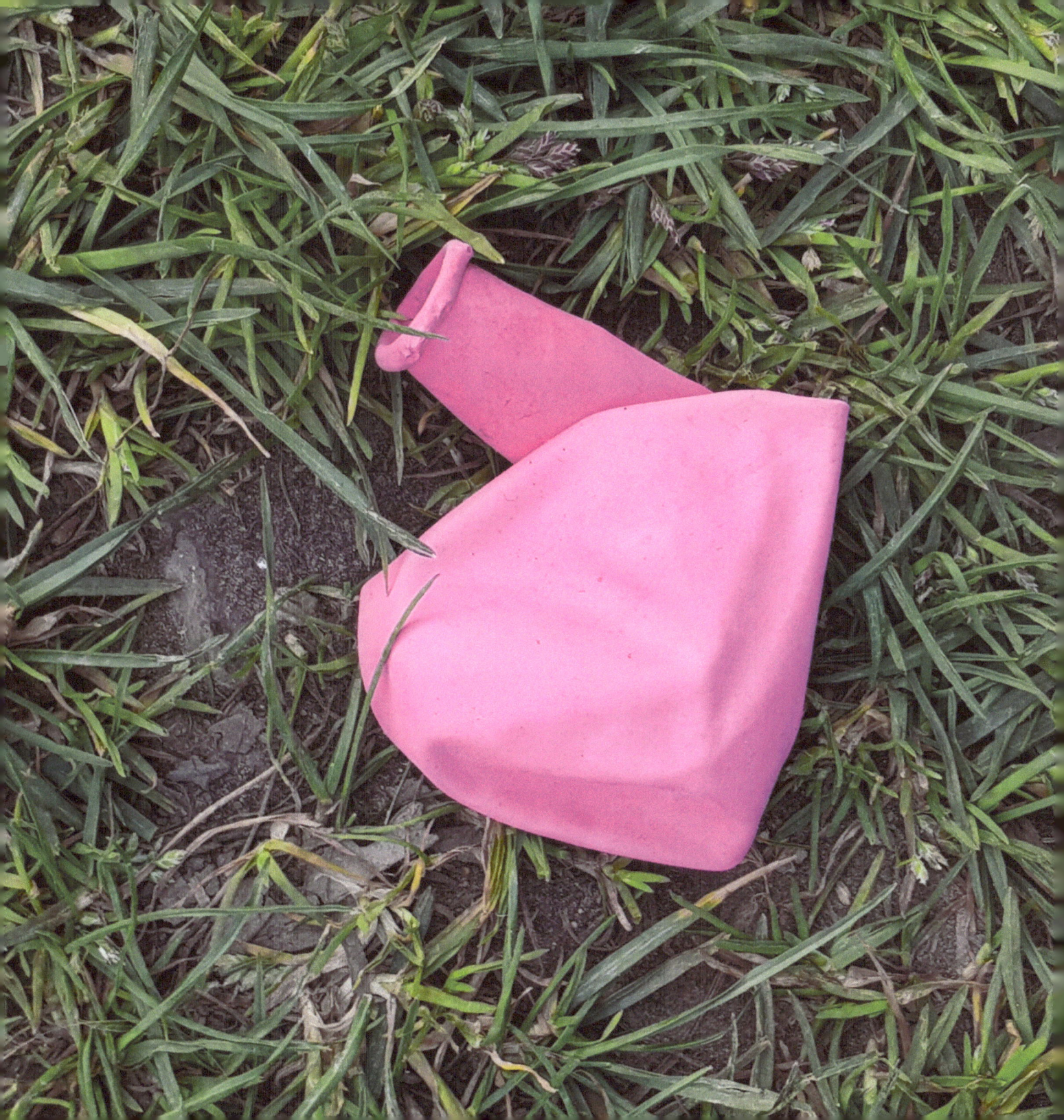

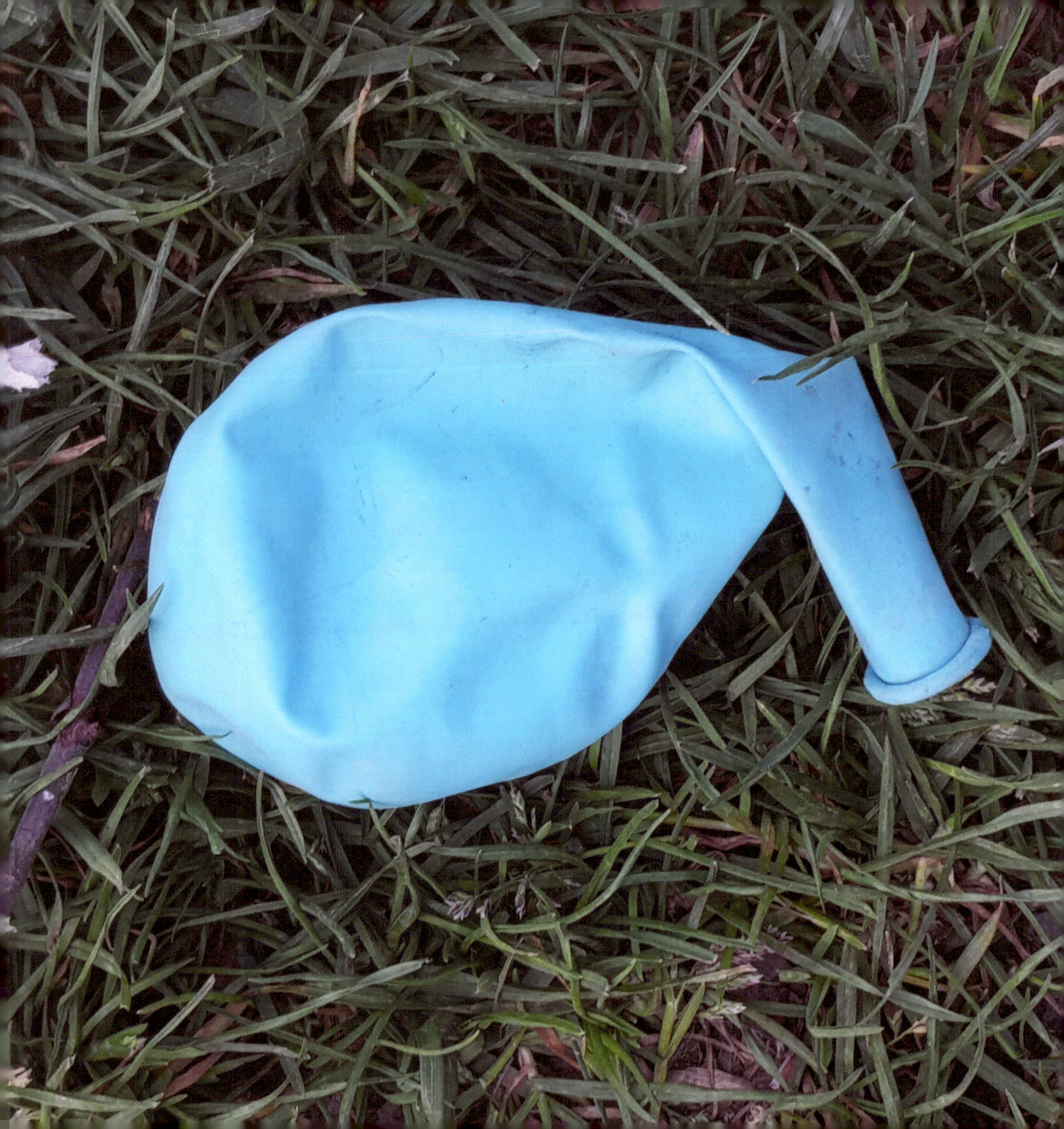

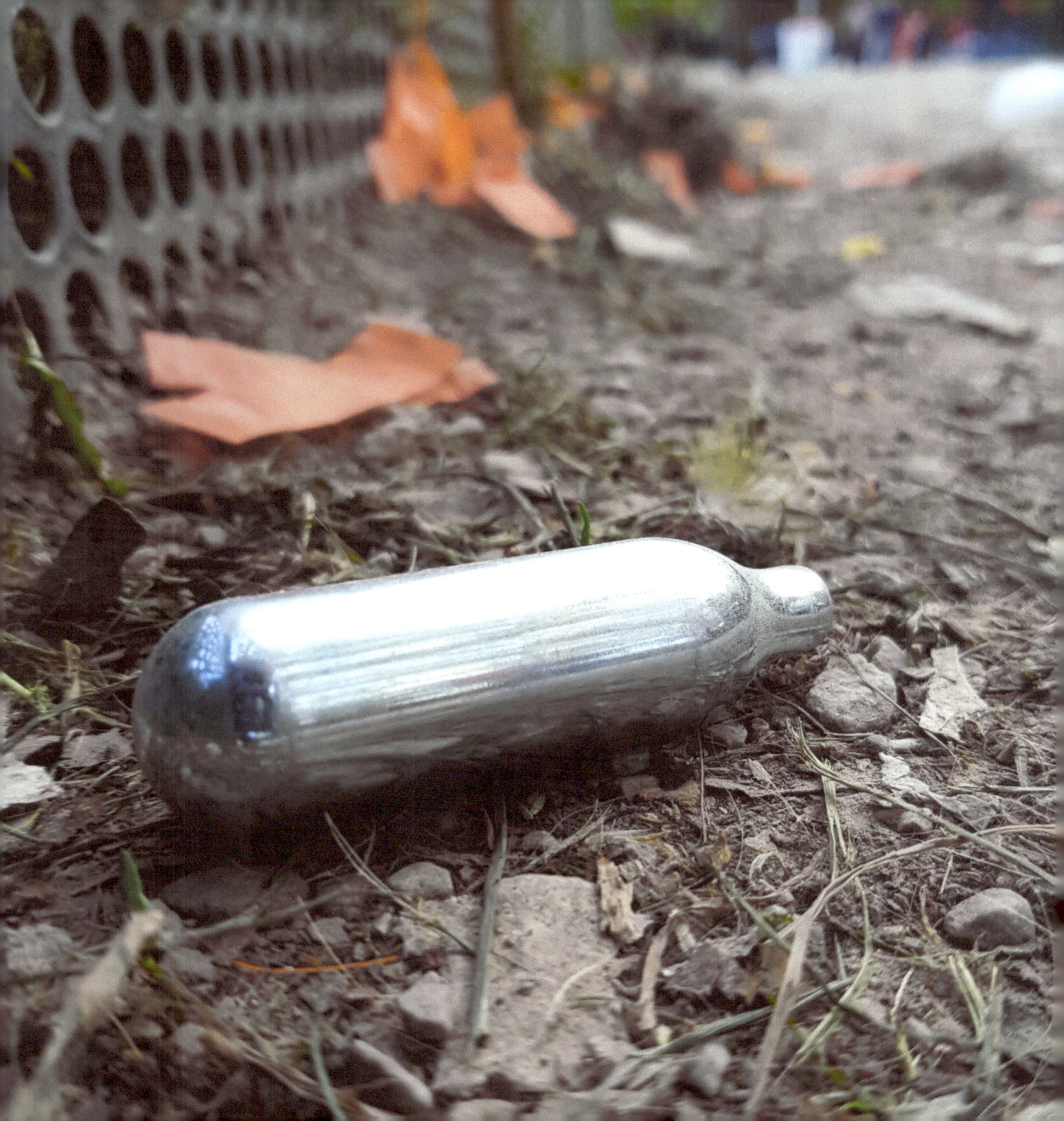

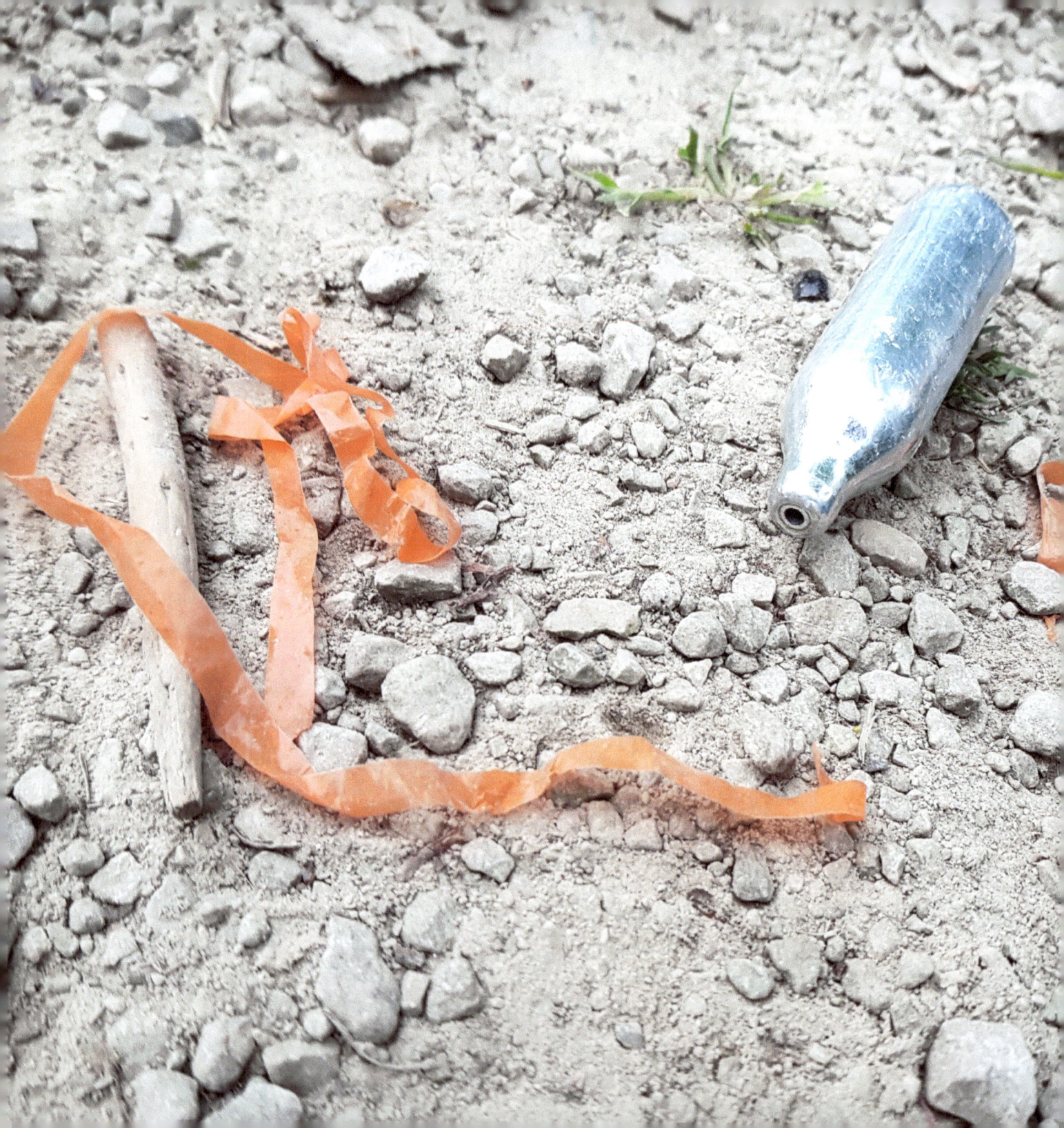

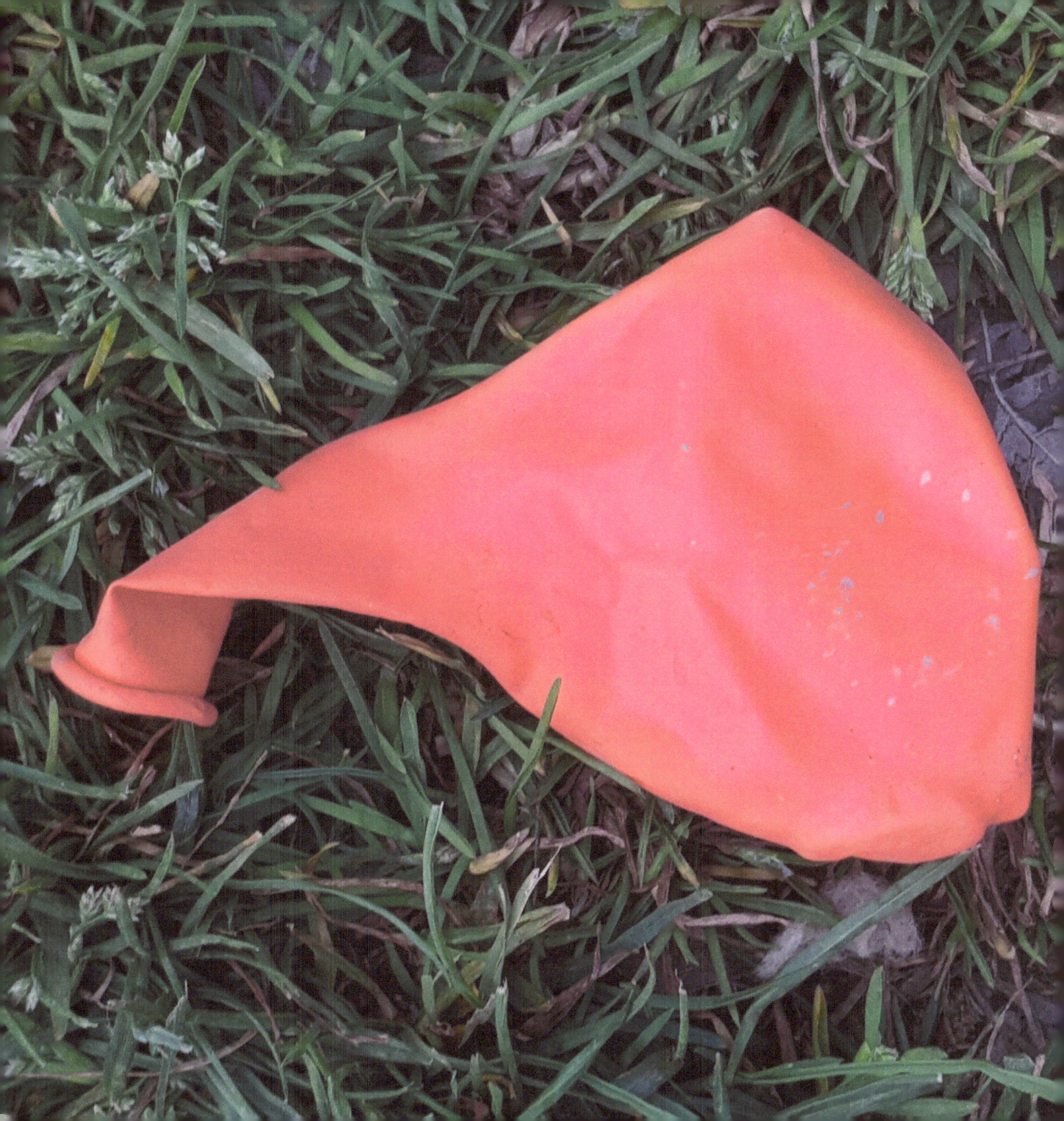

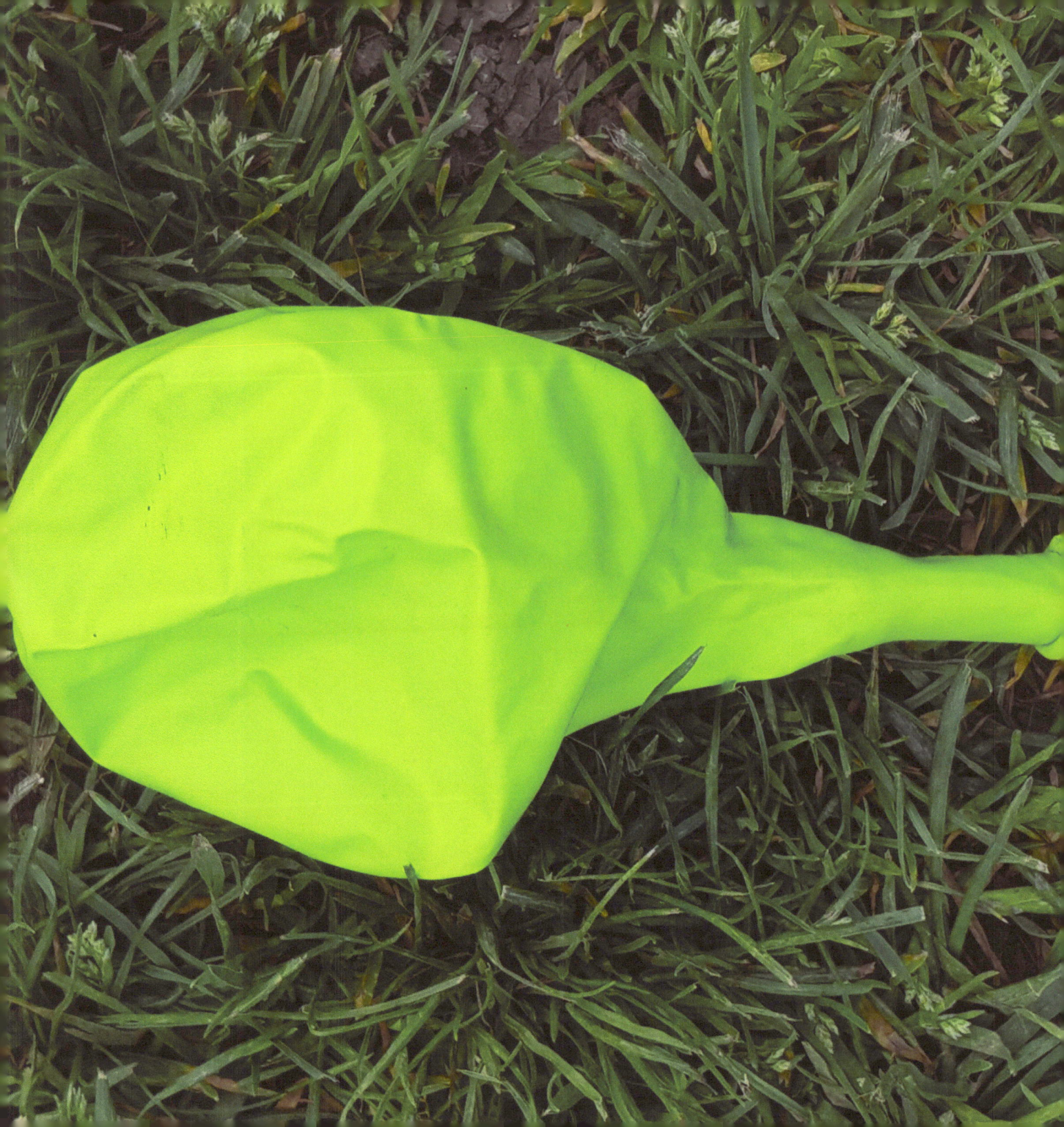

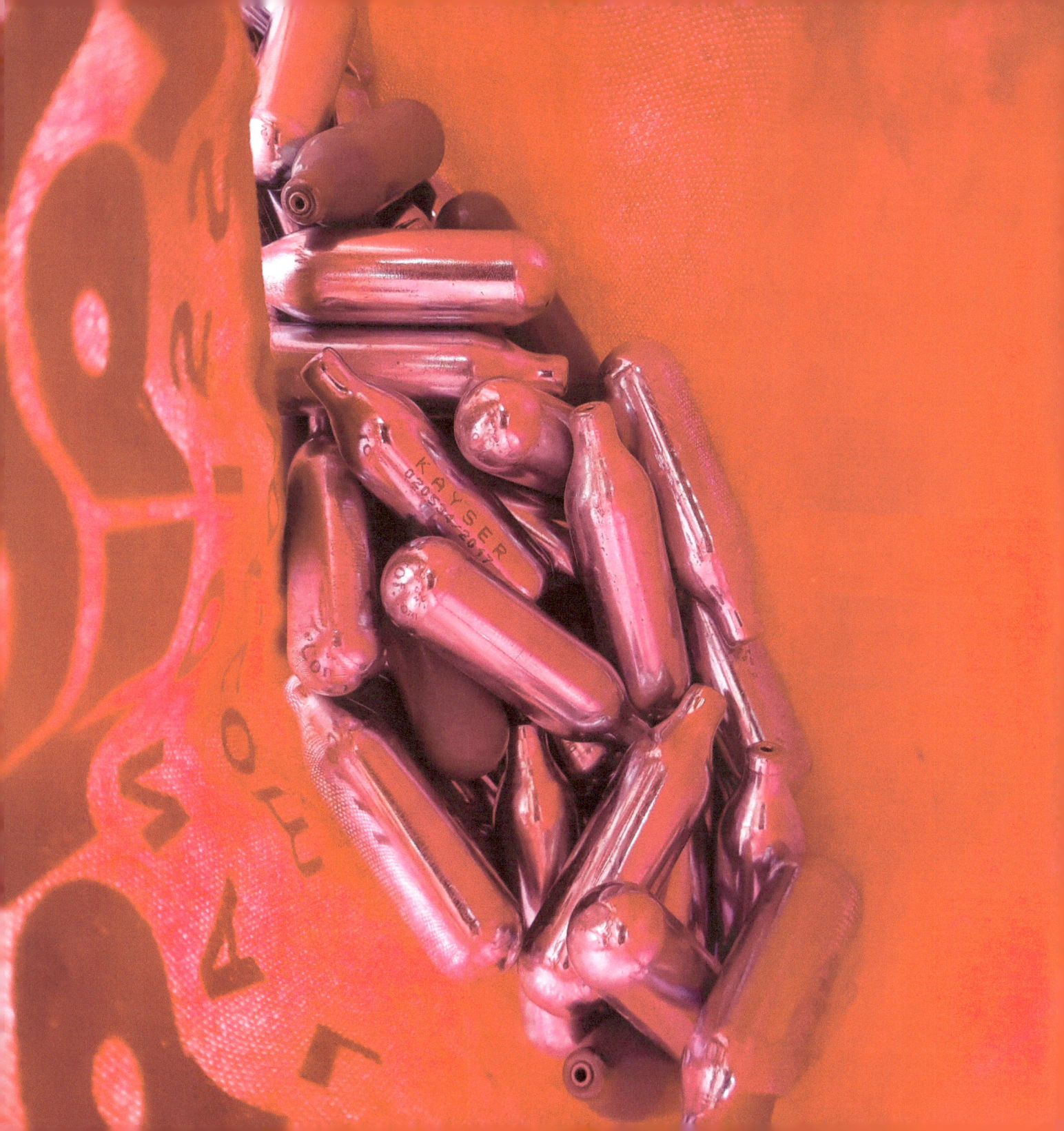

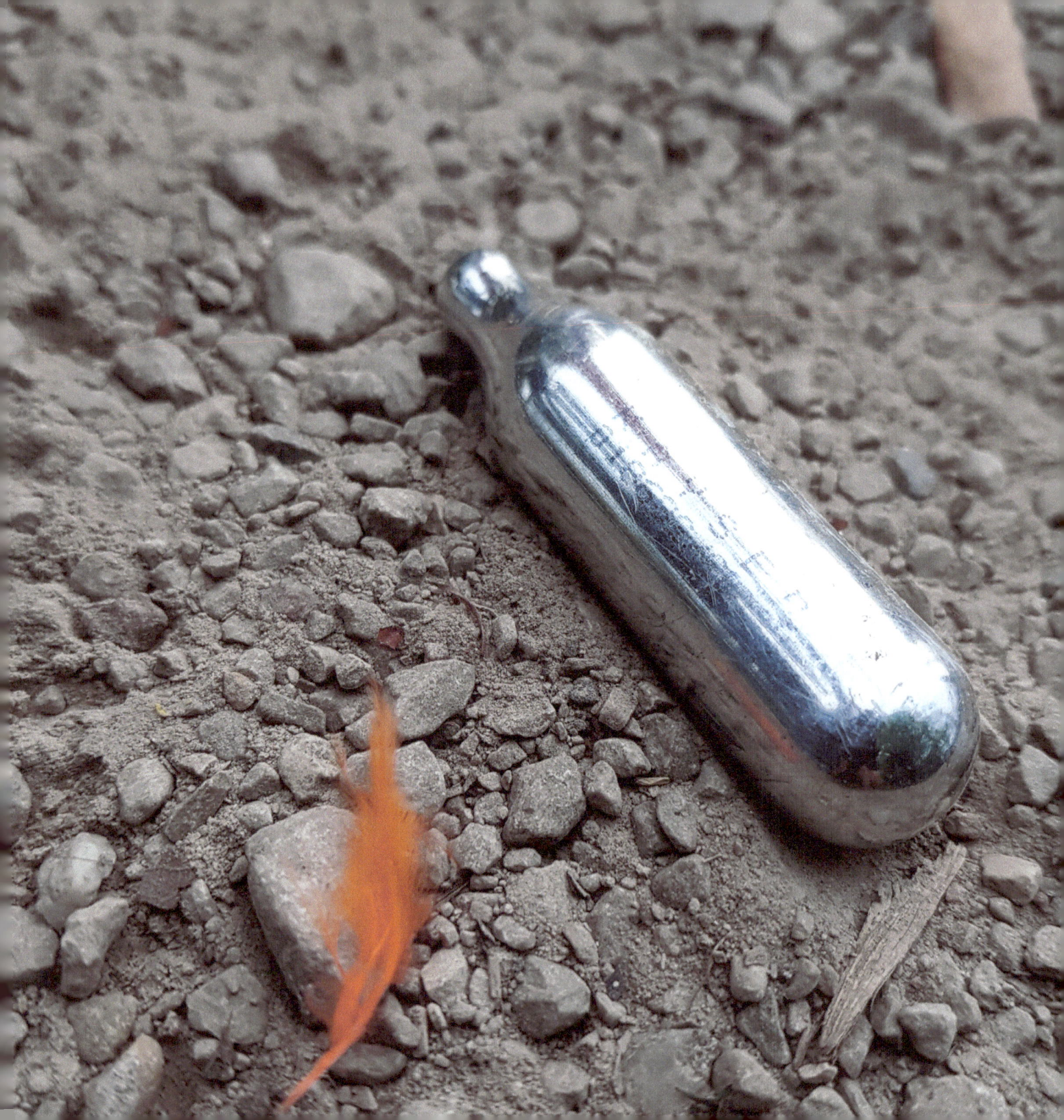

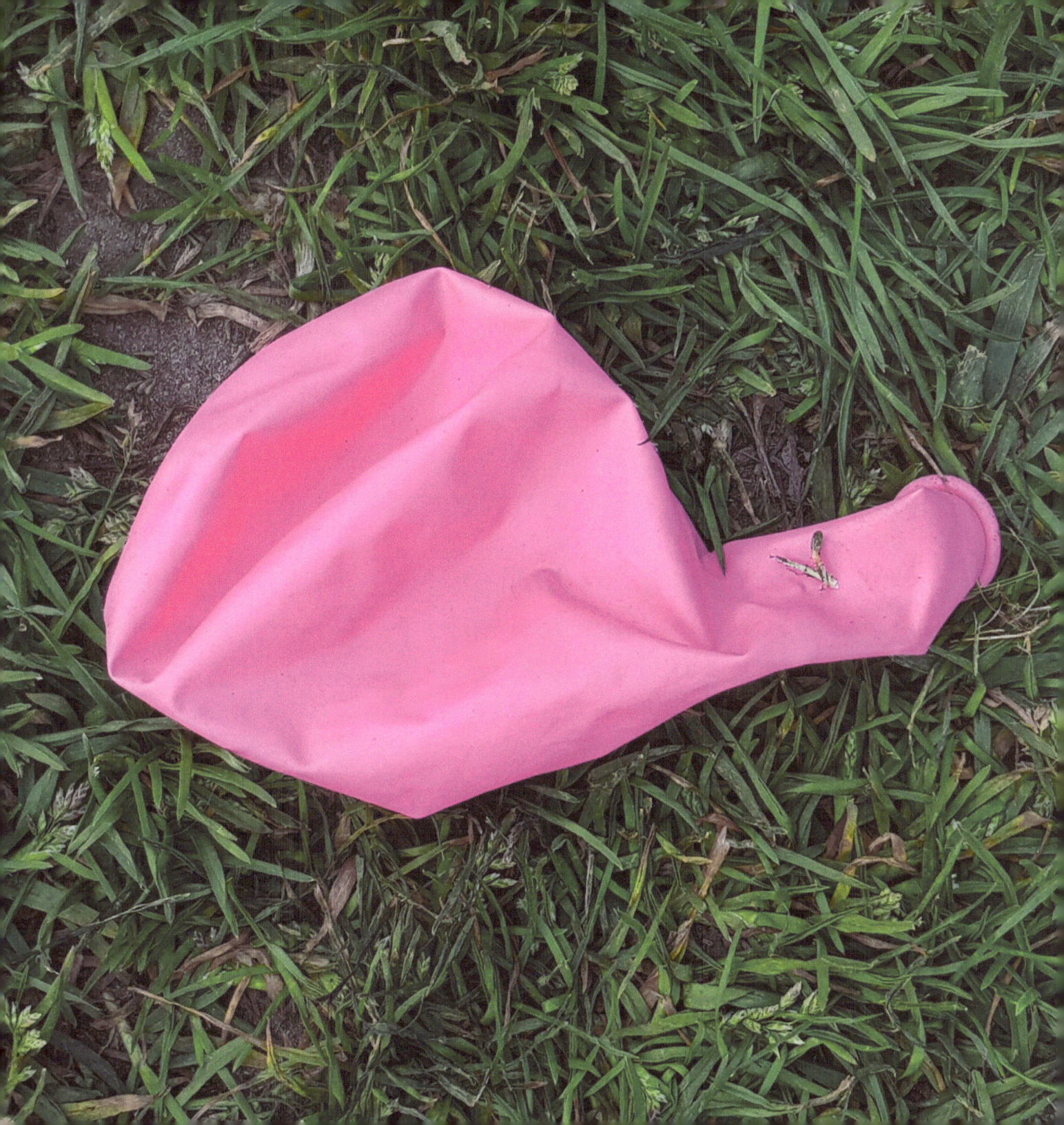

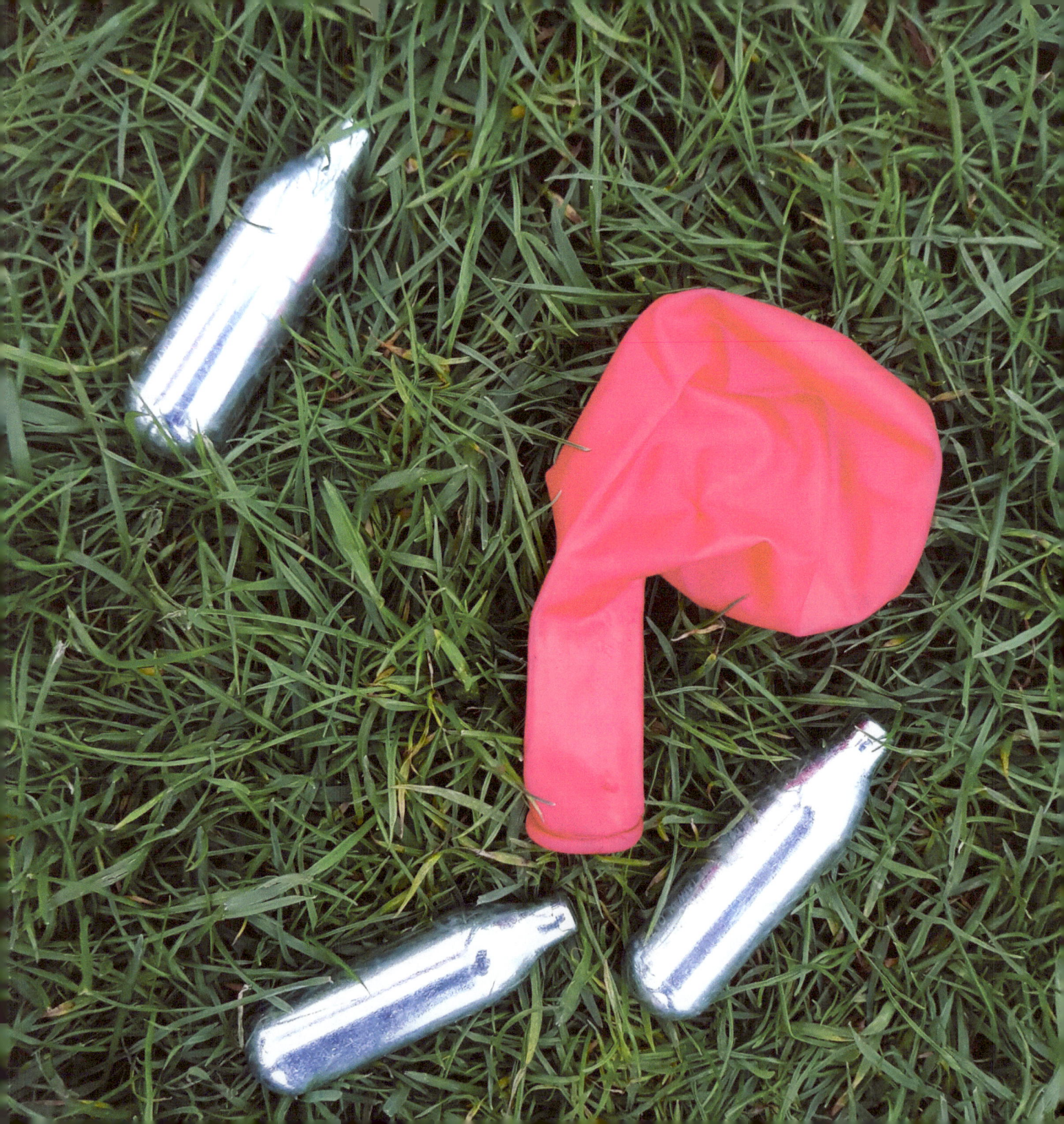

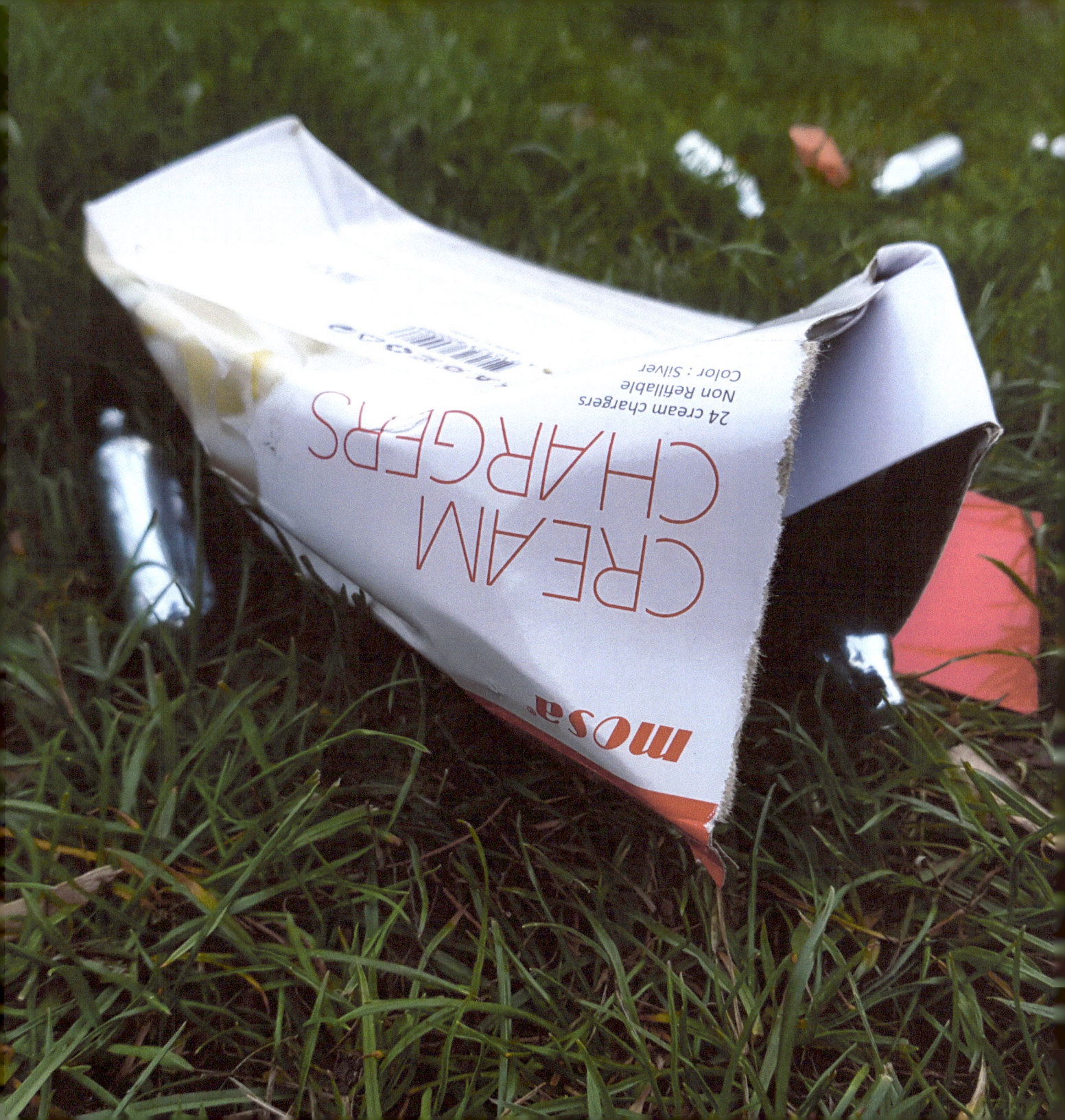

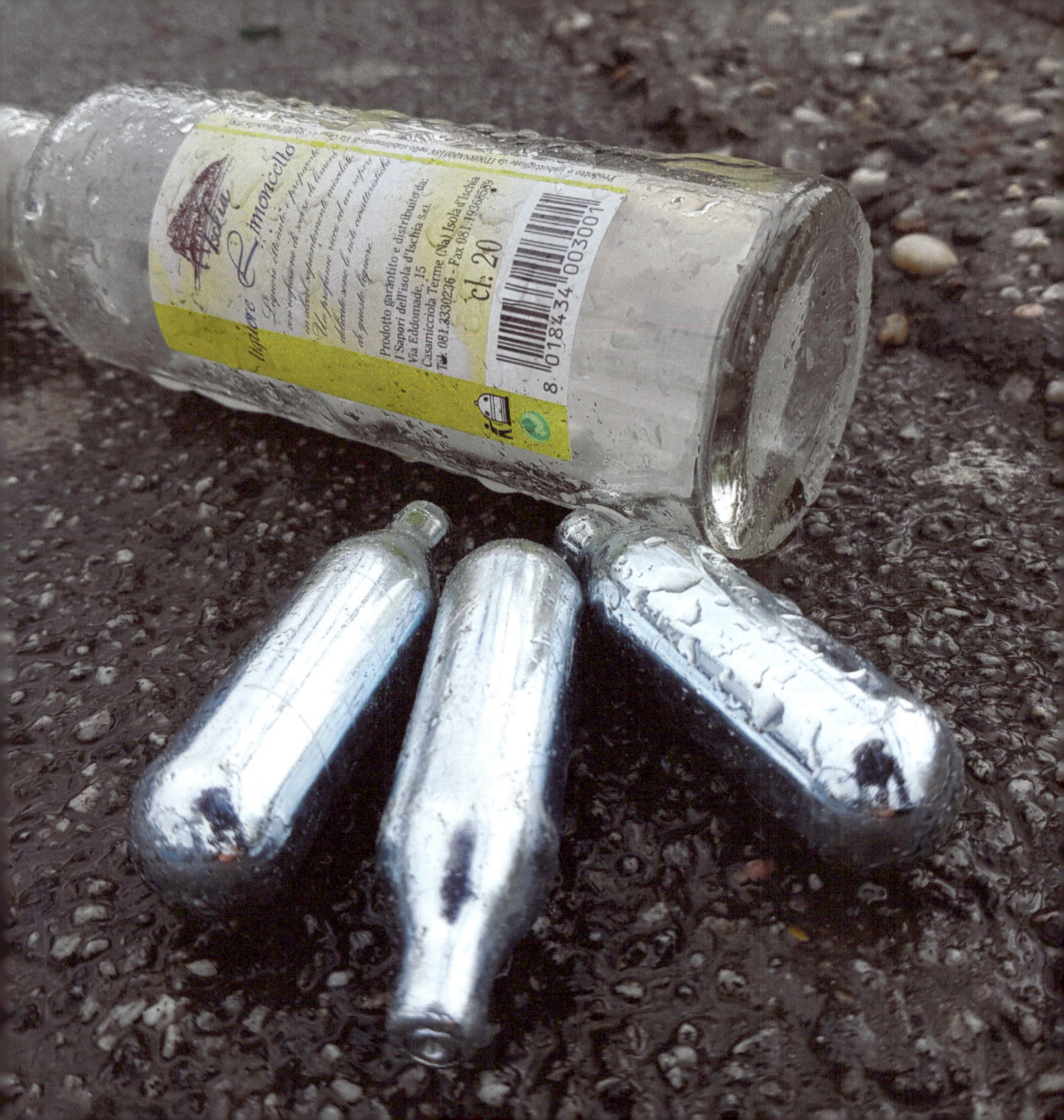

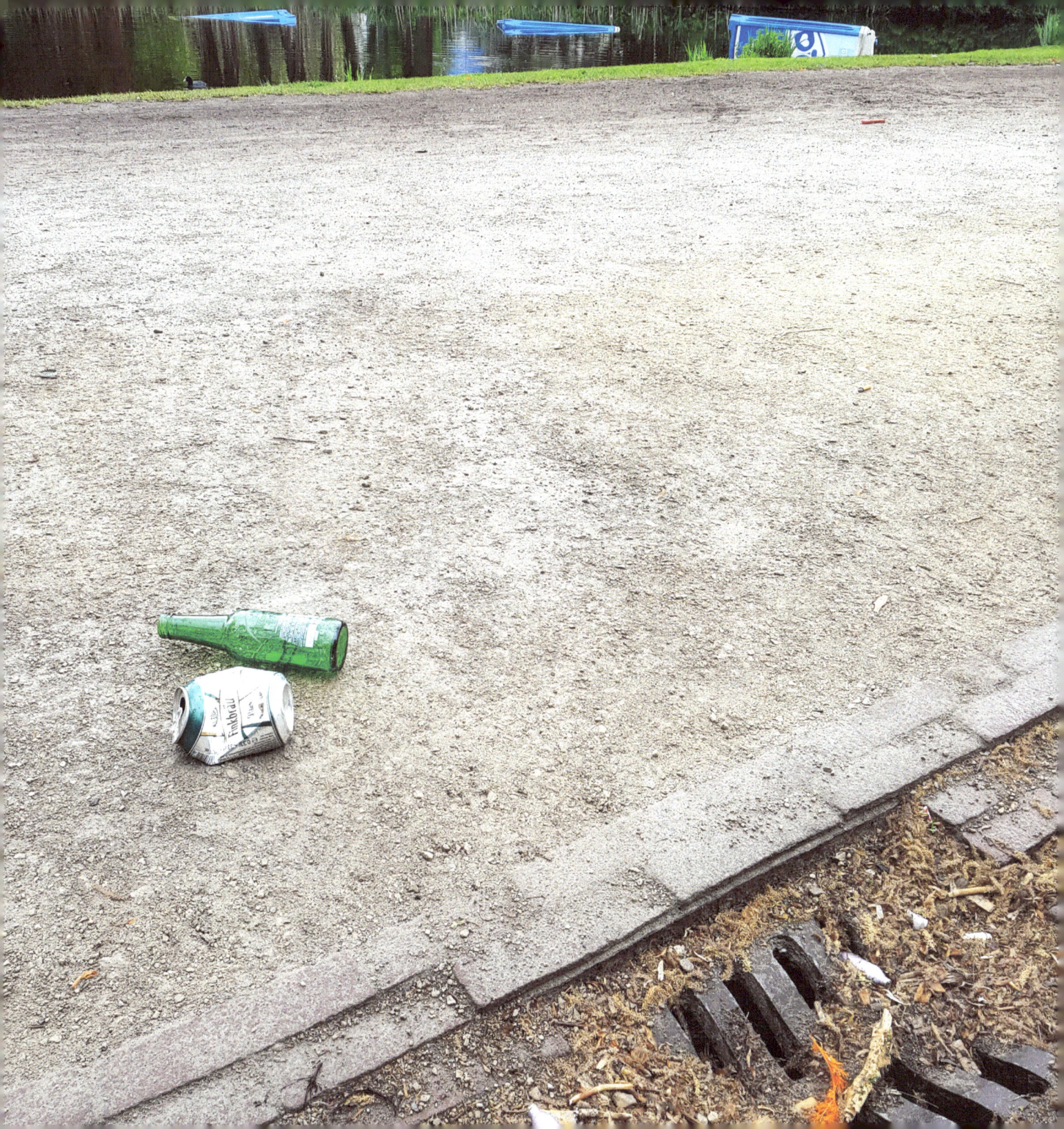

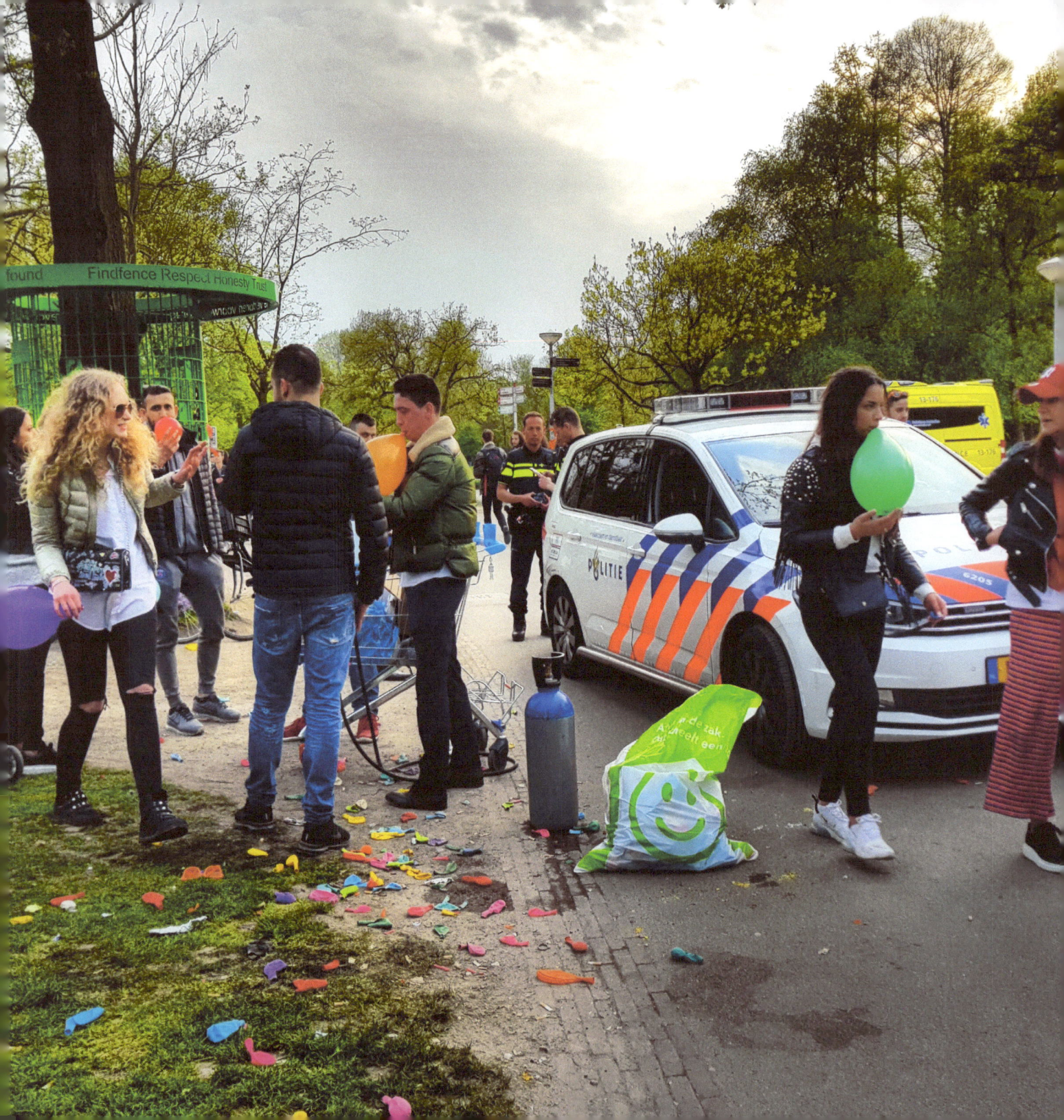

STOP THE POLLUTION & INSPIRE PEOPLE TO PICK-UP WHIPPED CREAM CANISTERS OF NITROUS OXIDE JUNKIES AND MAKE ART